G000055327

Microsoft®
Windows Vista
VISUAL™
Quick Tips

Visual®

by Paul McFedries

BICENTENNIAL
1807
WILEY
2007
BICENTENNIAL

Wiley Publishing, Inc.

Microsoft® Windows Vista™ VISUAL™ Quick Tips

Published by
Wiley Publishing, Inc.
111 River Street
Hoboken, NJ 07030-5774

Published simultaneously in Canada

Copyright © 2007 by Wiley Publishing, Inc.,
Indianapolis, Indiana

Library of Congress Control Number: 2006936746

ISBN: 978-0-470-04578-7

Manufactured in the United States of America

10 9 8 7 6 5 4 3 2 1

1K/QW/RS/QW/IN

Trademark Acknowledgments

Contact Us

For general information on our other products and services contact our Customer Care Department within the U.S. at 800-762-2974, outside the U.S. at 317-572-3993, or fax 317-572-4002.

For technical support, please visit www.wiley.com/techsupport.

Wiley Publishing, Inc.

Sales

Contact Wiley at (800) 762-2974 or fax (317) 572-4002.

Praise for Visual Books

"I have to praise you and your company on the fine products you turn out. I have twelve Visual books in my house. They were instrumental in helping me pass a difficult computer course. Thank you for creating books that are easy to follow. Keep turning out those quality books."

Gordon Justin (Brielle, NJ)

"What fantastic teaching books you have produced! Congratulations to you and your staff. You deserve the Nobel prize in Education. Thanks for helping me understand computers."

Bruno Tonon (Melbourne, Australia)

"A Picture Is Worth A Thousand Words! If your learning method is by observing or hands-on training, this is the book for you!"

Lorri Pegan-Durastante (Wickliffe, OH)

"Over time, I have bought a number of your 'Read Less - Learn More' books. For me, they are THE way to learn anything easily. I learn easiest using your method of teaching."

José A. Mazón (Cuba, NY)

"You've got a fan for life!! Thanks so much!!"

Kevin P. Quinn (Oakland, CA)

"I have several books from the Visual series and have always found them to be valuable resources."

Stephen P. Miller (Ballston Spa, NY)

"I have several of your Visual books and they are the best I have ever used."

Stanley Clark (Crawfordville, FL)

"Like a lot of other people, I understand things best when I see them visually. Your books really make learning easy and life more fun."

John T. Frey (Cadillac, MI)

"I have quite a few of your Visual books and have been very pleased with all of them. I love the way the lessons are presented!"

Mary Jane Newman (Yorba Linda, CA)

"Thank you, thank you, thank you...for making it so easy for me to break into this high-tech world."

Gay O'Donnell (Calgary, Alberta, Canada)

"I write to extend my thanks and appreciation for your books. They are clear, easy to follow, and straight to the point. Keep up the good work! I bought several of your books and they are just right! No regrets! I will always buy your books because they are the best."

Seward Kollie (Dakar, Senegal)

"I would like to take this time to thank you and your company for producing great and easy-to-learn products. I bought two of your books from a local bookstore, and it was the best investment I've ever made! Thank you for thinking of us ordinary people."

Jeff Eastman (West Des Moines, IA)

"Compliments to the chef!! Your books are extraordinary! Or, simply put, extra-ordinary, meaning way above the rest! THANK YOU THANK YOU THANK YOU! I buy them for friends, family, and colleagues."

Christine J. Manfrin (Castle Rock, CO)

Credits

Project Editor
Jade L. Williams

Acquisitions Editor
Jody Lefevere

Product Development Supervisor
Courtney Allen

Technical Editor
Lee Musick

Editorial Manager
Robyn Siesky

Business Manager
Amy Knies

Editorial Assistant
Laura Sinise

Manufacturing
Allan Conley
Linda Cook
Paul Gilchrist
Jennifer Guynn

Book Design
Kathie Rickard

Production Coordinator
Jennifer Theriot

Layout
Elizabeth Brooks
Jennifer Mayberry
Melanee Prendergast

Screen Artist
Jill A. Proll

Illustrators
Ronda David-Burroughs
Cheryl Grubbs

Cover Design
Anthony Bunyan

Proofreader
Jeannie Smith

Quality Control
Melanie Hoffman

Indexer
Lynnzee Elze

Special Help
Sarah Hellert
Jenny Watson

Vice President and Executive Group Publisher
Richard Swadley

Vice President and Publisher
Barry Pruett

Composition Director
Debbie Stailey

About the Author

Paul McFedries is the president of Logophilia Limited, a technical writing company. While now primarily a writer, Paul has worked as a programmer, consultant, and Web site developer. Paul has written nearly 50 books that have sold more than three million copies worldwide. These books include the Wiley titles *Windows XP: Top 100 Simplified Tips and Tricks,* 2nd Edition, and *Teach Yourself VISUALLY Computers,* 4th Edition. Paul also runs Word Spy, a Web site dedicated to tracking new words and phrases (see www.wordspy.com).

How To Use This Book

Microsoft Windows Vista VISUAL Quick Tips includes 92 tasks that reveal cool secrets, teach timesaving tricks, and explain great tips guaranteed to make you more productive with Windows Vista. The easy-to-use layout lets you work through all the tasks from beginning to end or jump in at random.

Who Is This Book For?

You already know Windows Vista basics. Now you'd like to go beyond, with shortcuts, tricks, and tips that let you work smarter and faster. And because you learn more easily when someone *shows* you how, this is the book for you.

Conventions Used In This Book

❶ Introduction

The introduction is designed to get you up to speed on the topic at hand.

❷ Steps

This book uses step-by-step instructions to guide you easily through each task. Numbered callouts on every screen shot show you exactly how to perform each task, step by step.

❸ Tips

Practical tips provide insights to save you time and trouble, caution you about hazards to avoid, and reveal how to do things with Windows Vista that you never thought possible!

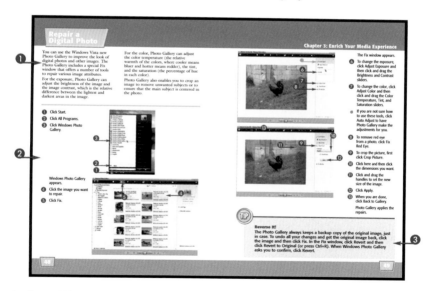

In order to get this information to you in a timely manner, this book was based on a pre-release version of Microsoft Vista/Microsoft Office 2007. There may be some minor changes between the screenshots in this book and what you see on your desktop. As always, Microsoft has the final word on how programs look and function; if you have any questions or see any discrepancies, consult the online help for further information about the software.

Table of Contents

chapter 3   **Enrich Your Media Experience**

chapter 4   **Get the Most Out of Your Files and Folders**

Make E-Mail Easier

chapter 8

Enhance Your Computer's Security and Privacy

Make Windows Vista Faster and More Efficient

Whether you use Windows Vista at work or at home, you probably want to spend your time on the computer creating documents, sending and receiving e-mail, browsing the Web, playing games, and doing other useful and fun activities. You probably do *not* want to spend your time wrestling with Windows Vista or waiting for it to finish its tasks.

Using a few simple techniques, you can make working with Windows Vista faster and more convenient. For example, rather than opening a number of Start menu folders to get to a program, you can create a shortcut in a more convenient location.

In addition, you can work with a few settings to ensure Windows Vista is working quickly and efficiently. For example, you can speed up your display by reducing the number of visual effects Windows Vista uses to draw screen elements.

Sometimes getting the most out of Windows Vista is a simple matter of taking care of the little details. For example, if you find yourself wasting precious time retyping errant text every time you accidentally press Caps Lock, you can avoid the problem altogether by setting up Windows Vista to warn you when you turn on Caps Lock.

Quick Tips

Create Shortcuts for Your Favorite Programs

If you have a program that you use regularly, you can access the program more quickly by creating a shortcut. A *shortcut* is a special file that points to a program. When you double-click the shortcut, Windows Vista automatically loads that program.

Shortcuts become particularly handy when you create them in a convenient location. For example, you can create a

program shortcut on your Windows Vista desktop. That way, instead of clicking the Start menu and opening a number of subfolders to find and launch a particular program, you can simply double-click the shortcut on the desktop.

You can create as many shortcuts as you want; the Windows Vista desktop offers a number of features that help you keep your shortcuts organized.

---

1 Right-click the location on your desktop where you want to create the shortcut.

2 Click New.

3 Click Shortcut.

The Create Shortcut wizard appears.

4 Click Browse.

The Browse for Files or Folders dialog box appears.

5 Select the program that you want the shortcut to start.

Note: *You can also create shortcuts to documents.*

6 Click OK.

7 Click Next.

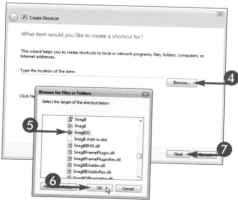

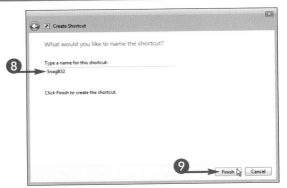

8 Type a name for the shortcut.

9 Click Finish.

● An icon for the shortcut appears on the desktop.

Note: *You can also pin shortcuts to your Start menu, as explained in "Pin an Item to Your Start Menu" in Chapter 2.*

Desktop Trick!

If you frequently use the Windows Vista desktop to store your program shortcuts, the desktop can quickly become a jumble of icons that make it difficult to find the shortcut you want. To solve this problem, right-click an empty spot on the desktop, click Sort By, and then click Name. This sorts the shortcuts alphabetically by name.

Adjust Visual Effects for Best Performance

You can turn off some or all of the visual effects that Windows Vista uses to display screen elements. This reduces the load on your computer, which improves the overall performance of your machine.

These visual effects include the animation Windows Vista uses when you minimize or maximize a window. For example, when you minimize a window, it appears to shrink down to the taskbar. Such effects are designed to help a novice user better understand what is happening on their computer.

Graphics performance is mostly determined by the amount of memory on your computer's graphics adapter. Most new computers have at least 32MB, so turning off visual effects will have little impact on performance. If your adapter has 8MB or less, turning off visual effects can improve performance.

① Click Start.

② Right-click Computer.

③ Click Properties.

The System window appears.

④ Click Advanced System Settings.

Note: If the User Account Control dialog box appears, click Continue or type an administrator password and click Submit.

The System Properties dialog box appears.

⑤ Click the Advanced tab.

⑥ In the Performance area, click Settings.

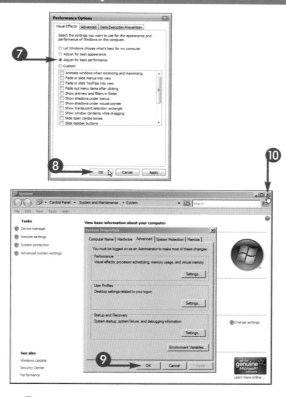

The Performance Options dialog box appears.

7 Click the Adjust for best performance option (○ changes to ⦿).

8 Click OK to return to the System Properties dialog box.

Windows Vista turns off the visual effects.

9 Click OK.

The System Properties dialog box closes.

10 Click the Close box.

Did You Know?

If you do not know how much memory your graphics adapter has, Windows Vista can tell you. Follow steps **1** to **3** to display the System window, and then click the Windows Experience Index link. In the Performance Information and Tools window that appears, click the View and print details link. The Dedicated graphics memory value tells you the amount of memory in your graphics adapter.

Ensure Windows Vista Is Optimized for Programs

You can set an option that ensures Windows Vista maximizes the performance of your programs. This option controls processor scheduling in Windows Vista.

The *processor* (or *CPU*) is the chip inside your machine that coordinates all the computer's activity; some call it the brain of the computer. *Processor scheduling*

determines how much time the processor allocates to the computer's activities. In particular, processor scheduling differentiates between the *foreground program* — the program in which you are currently working — and *background programs* — programs that perform tasks, such as printing or backing up, while you work in another program.

① Click Start.

② Right-click Computer.

③ Click Properties.

The System window appears.

④ Click Advanced System Settings.

Note: *If the User Account Control dialog box appears, click Continue or type an administrator password and click Submit.*

The System Properties dialog box appears.

⑤ Click the Advanced tab.

⑥ In the Performance area, click Settings.

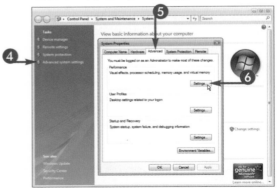

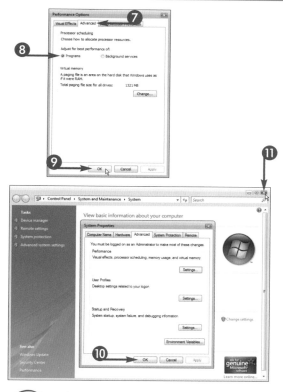

The Performance Options dialog box appears.

⑦ Click the Advanced tab.

⑧ In the Processor scheduling area, click the Programs option (◯ changes to ◉).

⑨ Click OK to return to the System Properties dialog box.

Windows Vista applies the performance settings.

⑩ Click OK.

⑪ Click the Close box.

The System Properties dialog box closes.

Did You Know?

If you do not know what kind of processor or how much memory your computer has, Windows Vista can tell you. Follow steps **1** to **3** to display the System window, and then click the Windows Experience Index link. In the Performance Information and Tools window that appears, click the View and print details link. In the Details column, read the Processor and Memory (RAM) values.

Improve Performance with a USB Flash Drive

If you add a USB flash drive to your computer, Windows Vista can use the memory on that drive to improve the performance of your system.

Windows Vista uses a technology named SuperFetch to boost system performance. SuperFetch tracks the programs and data you use over time to create a kind of profile of your hard drive usage. Using this profile, SuperFetch can then anticipate the data that you might use in the near future. It would then load (fetch) that data into memory ahead of time.

If you elect to insert a USB 2.0 flash drive (memory key) into your system to speed up your system, SuperFetch will use that drive's capacity as storage for the data that SuperFetch anticipates you will require.

SPEED UP YOUR SYSTEM

①	Insert a flash drive into a USB port on your computer.

	The AutoPlay dialog box appears.

②	Click the Speed up my system using this device option.

	Windows Vista configures SuperFetch to use the flash drive's memory.

CONFIGURE FLASH DRIVE MEMORY

①	Click Start.

②	Click Computer.

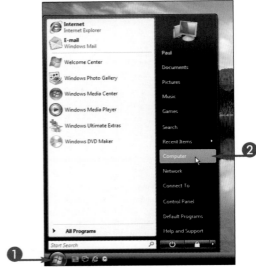

The Computer window appears.

③ Click the flash drive icon.

④ Click Properties.

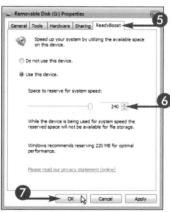

The drive's Properties dialog box appears.

⑤ Click the ReadyBoost tab.

⑥ Click and drag the slider, or click the Spinner arrows, to set the amount of drive memory Vista sets aside for SuperFetch.

⑦ Click OK.

Reverse It!

If you decide later on that you want to use the flash drive's full capacity for file storage, you can tell Windows Vista not to use the drive to augment SuperFetch. Click Start, Computer, click the flash drive, and then click Properties. Click the ReadyBoost tab and then click the Do not use this device option (○ changes to ◉). Click OK to put the new setting into effect.

Run a Program with Elevated Privileges

If you need to perform advanced tasks in a program, you may need to run that program with elevated privileges.

With Windows Vista's User Account Control, you must provide credentials to perform certain actions. However, this security model falls short when you need to perform certain actions. For example, if you edit a file in one of the Windows Vista protected folders, you will receive a Permission Denied error when you try to save your changes.

To work around such problems, you need to start the program you are using with elevated privileges. This tells Windows Vista to run the program as though you were using the Administrator account, the highest-level account on your system, and the only account that does not need to provide credentials.

---

① Click Start.

② Click All Programs.

③ Click the Start menu folder that contains the icon of the program you want to run.

● For example, to run the Command Prompt with elevated privileges, click Accessories.

④ Right-click the program icon (for example, the Command Prompt icon).

⑤ Click Run as administrator.

The User Account Control dialog box appears.

⑥ Click Continue.

If you have a standard user account, type the password for an administrator and then click Submit.

Windows Vista runs the program with elevated privileges.

Did You Know?

If you have a program that you use frequently and you normally run it with elevated privileges, you can tell Windows Vista to always run the program elevated. Follow steps **1** to **3** in this task to find the program icon, right-click the icon, and then click Properties. Click the Compatibility tab, click the Run this program as an administrator check box (☐ changes to ☑), and then click OK.

Make Your File Searches Run Faster

You can add folders to the Windows Search engine's index, which makes your file searches in those folders run noticeably faster.

The Windows Vista Search feature works well if what you are looking for is in your main user account folder or one of its subfolders (such as Documents, Pictures, and Music). This is because Windows Vista automatically *indexes* those folders, which means it keeps a detailed record of the contents of all your files.

If you have files in a different location, Windows Vista does not index them, which makes searching for those files very time-consuming. You can dramatically speed up the searching of those files by adding their location to the Search index.

---

① Click Start.

② Click Control Panel.

The Control Panel window appears.

③ Click System and Maintenance.

The System and Maintenance window appears.

④ Click Indexing Options.

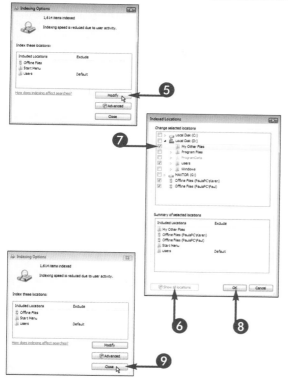

The Indexing Options dialog box appears.

⑤ Click Modify.

⑥ Click Show all locations.

Note: If the User Account Control dialog box appears, click Continue or type an administrator password and click Submit.

⑦ Click the folder you want to include in the index.

● The folder appears in the list of included locations.

⑧ Click OK.

⑨ Click Close.

Windows Vista includes the folder in the index and begins rebuilding the index.

Note: To learn how to run advanced searches in Windows Vista, see "Perform an Advanced File Search" in Chapter 4.

Did You Know?
If Windows Vista takes a long time to search or cannot find your files, you may need to rebuild the index. Follow steps **1** to **5** to display the Indexing Options dialog box and activate the global settings. Click Advanced to display the Advanced Options dialog box, and then click Rebuild.

You can adjust a setting that tells Windows Vista to beep your computer's speaker whenever you press the Caps Lock key.

When you are typing quickly, it is common to accidentally press the Caps Lock key instead of either Shift, Tab, or A. As you probably know, when you inadvertently press Caps Lock, it may be a while before you realize it. This means that you end up with a great deal of typing that has the capital letters reversed. Not only must you delete this text, but you must also retype it with the correct letters, all of which wastes valuable time.

To save this wasted time, you can configure Windows Vista to beep your computer's speaker when you press Caps Lock.

① Click Start.

② Click Control Panel.

The Control Panel window appears.

③ Click Ease of Access.

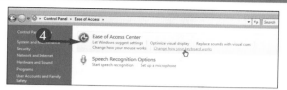

The Ease of Access Center window appears.

④ Click Change how your keyboard works.

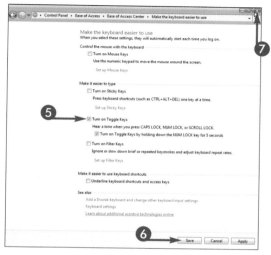

⑤ Click the Turn on Toggle Keys check box
(☐ changes to ☑).

⑥ Click Save.

⑦ Click the Close box to close the Ease of Access Center window.

Windows alerts you with a tone when you press the Caps Lock key.

Did You Know?

You can turn off Toggle Keys by holding down the Num Lock key for five seconds, until you hear a beep. To turn it back on, hold down Num Lock for five seconds, until you see the Toggle Keys dialog box. Click OK to turn Toggle Keys on; click Cancel to leave Toggle Keys off.

Display More Programs On Your Start Menu

You can customize the Start menu to display more of the programs you use most often.

The list displaying your most frequently used programs appears on the bottom-left side of the Start menu, above All Programs. As you work with your programs, Windows Vista keeps track of how many times you launch each one. The programs that you have launched most often appear on the Start menu for

easy, two-click access. These programs appear at the top of the list, followed by the next most-often-used programs, and so on. When another program becomes popular, Windows Vista drops the bottom program and adds the new one.

The default Start menu shows just the six most popular programs, but you can increase the size of the list to force Windows Vista to display more programs.

---

1 Right-click Start.

2 Click Properties.

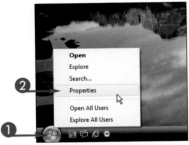

The Taskbar and Start Menu Properties dialog box appears.

3 Click the Start Menu tab.

4 Click Customize.

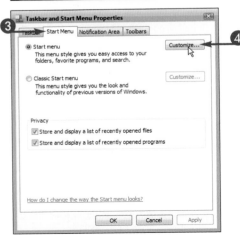

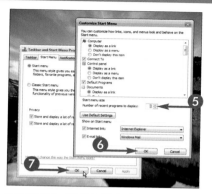

The Customize Start Menu dialog box appears.

⑤ Type the number of programs you want to see.

Note: *The maximum number of programs is 30.*

⑥ Click OK to return to the Taskbar and Start Menu Properties dialog box.

⑦ Click OK.

● Windows Vista adjusts the size of the Start menu's most frequently used program list.

More Options!
The height of the Start menu is restricted by the height of your screen. To display more Start menu items without changing the screen height, follow steps **1** to **4** to open the Customize Start Menu dialog box. In the list, click to uncheck the Use large icons check box (☑ changes to ☐), and then click OK. Using smaller icons enables more items to appear on the Start menu.

Launch Control Panel Icons Faster by Using a Menu

You can quickly access items in the Control Panel by converting the Start menu's Control Panel item into a menu.

The longer you use Windows Vista, the more you appreciate the Control Panel. The problem, however, is that the default Control Panel window uses a category view that groups the Control Panel icons into categories, such as System and

Maintenance, Security, and Appearance and Personalization. That view hampers more experienced users, who must often negotiate several windows to get to the icon they want. Converting the Start menu's Control Panel item into a menu on the Start menu enables you to easily find and choose any Control Panel item.

① Right-click Start.

② Click Properties.

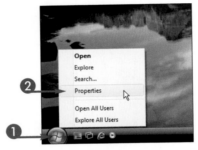

The Taskbar and Start Menu Properties dialog box appears.

③ Click the Start Menu tab.

④ Click Customize.

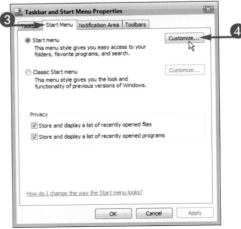

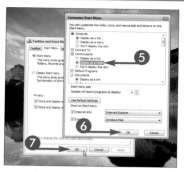

The Customize Start Menu dialog box appears.

5 In the list of Start menu items, under Control Panel, click the Display as a menu option (○ changes to ◉).

6 Click OK to return to the Taskbar and Start Menu Properties dialog box.

7 Click OK.

8 Click Start.

9 Click Control Panel.

● A menu of the Control Panel items appears.

● If the entire menu does not fit on your screen, position the mouse here to expand the menu.

More Options!
You can display other Start menu items as menus. Follow steps **1** to **5** to display the Customize Start Menu dialog box. The following branches have a Display as a menu option that you can click (○ changes to ◉): Computer, Documents, Games, Music, Personal folder, and Pictures.

Update a Device Driver to Ensure Top Device Performance

You can ensure that a device is working at optimum performance by updating the device's driver to the latest version.

Windows Vista communicates with a hardware device by using a small program called a *device driver*, and this communication works two ways: from the device and to the device. For example, a keyboard uses its device driver to let Windows Vista know which key you pressed.

Hardware manufacturers often create new versions of their device drivers to fix problems and improve the device's performance. For these reasons, it is a good idea to always use the latest device drivers for your system's hardware. After you download a new driver from the manufacturer's Web site, you then need to update the existing driver on your system.

---

① Click Start.

② Click Control Panel.

The Control Panel window appears.

③ Click System and Maintenance.

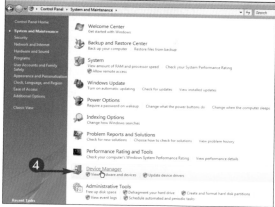

The System and Maintenance window appears.

④ Click Device Manager.

Note: If the User Account Control dialog box appears, click Continue or type an administrator password and click Submit.

The Device Manager window appears.

⑤ Click the device you want to update.

Did You Know?

If you have a device that is performing slowly or is having problems, the cause may be a corrupted device driver file. In most cases, you can fix this problem by reinstalling the device's driver. Follow the steps in this task and, when it is time to select the driver, select the original driver, which is usually on the CD that came with the device.

Most device manufacturers offer a Web site where you can download the latest drivers, but it helps to know how to navigate these sites.

Look for an area of the site dedicated to driver downloads. The good sites have links to areas named Downloads or Drivers, but it is far more common to go through a Support or Customer Service area first.

When you get to the device's download page, be careful which file you choose. Make sure that it is a Windows Vista driver, and make sure that you are not downloading a utility program or some other non-driver file.

When you finally get to download the file, save it to your computer. The best location is your user account's Downloads folder.

---

6 Click the Update Driver Software button.

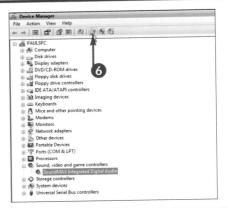

The Update Driver Software dialog box appears.

7 Click Browse my computer for driver software.

Note: *If you have a CD with the device driver, insert the disc and click Search automatically for updated driver software, instead.*

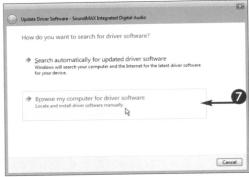

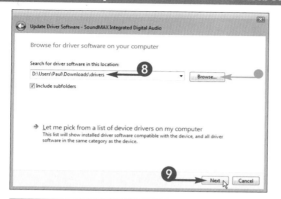

The Browse for driver software on your computer dialog box appears.

⑧ Type the location of the folder where you saved the downloaded driver.

● Alternatively, click Browse, use the Browse for Folder dialog box to select the folder, and then click OK.

⑨ Click Next.

Windows Vista installs the driver.

⑩ Click Close.

⑪ Click the Close box to close Device Manager.

Windows Vista now uses the updated device driver.

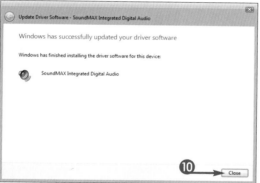

Reverse It!

The latest device drivers are usually the most stable and bug-free. However, you may occasionally find that updating a device driver causes problems. In that case, you need to *roll back* the driver to the previous version. Follow steps **1** to **4** to display Device Manager, and then double-click your device. Click the Driver tab and then click the Roll Back Driver button.

Set Up Windows Vista the Way You Want

Windows Vista is endlessly customizable and offers many features that enable you to modify the look and feel of your system to suit your style and the way you work.

Although changing your screen colors might make Windows Vista more interesting, it does not help you get your work done any faster. However, a technique such as revamping your Start menu for easy access to your most-used programs can save you lots of mouse clicks and, ultimately, lots of time.

This chapter focuses on the practical aspects of customizing Windows Vista by showing you a number of techniques, most

of which are designed to save you time and make Windows Vista more efficient. You begin with several techniques that make your Start menu much easier to deal with, including adding icons permanently, removing unneeded icons, and putting the Run command on the Start menu.

Other techniques in this chapter include displaying clocks for other time zones, adding program icons to the handy Quick Launch toolbar, hiding the taskbar to get more screen space, getting older programs to run in Windows Vista, configuring the Windows Vista default behavior when you insert CDs, and customizing the icons in the notification area.

Quick Tips

Pin an Item to Your Start Menu

The items on the main Start menu — including Computer, Internet, E-mail — are very handy because they require just two clicks to launch. To start up all your other programs, you must also click All Programs and then negotiate one or more submenus. For those programs you use most often, you can avoid this extra work by *pinning* their icons permanently to the main Start menu.

All pinned program items appear on the left side of the Start menu, in the top section where the Internet and E-mail icons reside. If you have pinned several programs and you find this section is getting too crowded, you can remove a pinned item by right-clicking the item and then clicking Unpin from the Start menu.

---

① Click Start.

② Click All Programs.

Note: *After you click All Programs, the name changes to Back.*

③ If necessary, click the submenu that contains the program you want to pin to the Start menu. For example, if the program is in the Accessories submenu, click Accessories.

④ Right-click the program icon.

⑤ Click Pin to Start Menu.

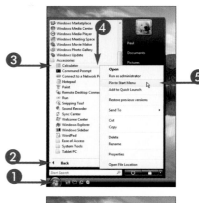

● Windows Vista adds the program to the main Start menu.

● You can also use the same technique to pin any of the often-used program items to the main Start menu.

The left side of the main Start menu is divided into two sections. The top part consists of menu items that remain in place, including the Internet and E-mail icons and any pinned program items. The bottom part consists of shortcuts to the eight programs that you have used most often, so this will change as you use your computer. You can remove shortcuts for

programs that you no longer use from either section on the left side of the Start menu.

You can also delete items from the All Programs menu and its various submenus. To do this, click Start, All Programs, and then open the menu that contains the item you want to delete. Right-click the item and then click Delete.

① Click Start.

② Right-click the item you want to remove.

③ Click Remove from this list.

● Windows Vista removes the item from the Start menu.

Note: To learn how to show more programs on the Start menu, see "Display More Programs on the Start Menu" in Chapter 1.

Add the Run Command to the Start Menu

If you often use the Run dialog box to open programs, folders, and Web sites, you can make the dialog box much easier to launch by adding the Run command to the main Start menu.

The Run dialog box is a very handy tool, but if you use it frequently, you will be disappointed to find out that Windows Vista buries the Run command in the Accessories menu (select Start, All Programs, Accessories, and then Run). This is inconvenient and time-consuming. However, you can fix this problem by customizing Windows Vista to display the Run command on the main Start menu. This enables you to open the Run dialog box with just a couple of mouse clicks.

① **Right-click Start.**

② **Click Properties.**

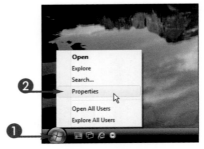

The Taskbar and Start Menu Properties dialog box appears.

③ **Click the Start Menu tab.**

④ **Click Customize.**

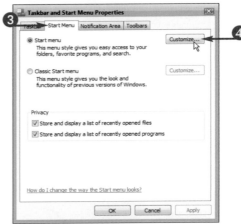

The Customize Start Menu dialog box appears.

5 Click the Run command check box (☐ changes to ☑).

6 Click OK.

7 Click OK.

8 Click Start.

● Windows Vista adds the Run command to the Start menu.

TIP

Did You Know?

If your Windows Vista Start menu is already overcrowded, you might not want to add the Run command. One solution is to remove other Start menu items you do not use by following steps **1** to **4** and then deactivate the check boxes for the items you want to remove. Alternatively, leave Run off the main Start menu and launch the Run dialog box by pressing Windows Logo key+R.

If you deal with people in another time zone, you can make it easier to find out the current time in that zone by customizing Windows Vista to show a second clock that is configured for the time zone.

If you have colleagues, friends, or family members in a different time zone, it is often important to know the correct time in that zone. For example, you would not want to call someone at home at 9 AM your time if that person lives in a time zone that is three hours behind you.

If you need to verify the current time in another time zone, you can customize the Windows Vista date and time display to show the current time in the other time zone.

① Right-click the time.

② Click Adjust Date/Time.

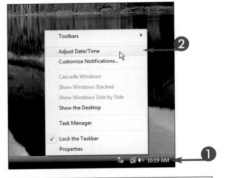

The Date and Time dialog box appears.

③ Click the Additional Clocks tab.

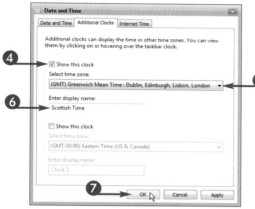

④ Click the Show this clock check box (☐ changes to ☑).

⑤ Click here and select the time zone you want to use in the new clock.

⑥ Type a name for the new clock.

⑦ Click OK.

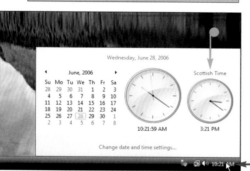

Windows Vista adds the clock.

⑧ Click the time.

● Windows Vista displays the extra clock.

Did You Know?

After you customize Windows Vista with the extra clock, you normally click the time in the notification area to see both clocks. However, if you just hover the mouse pointer over the time, Windows Vista displays a banner that shows the current date, your current local time, and the current time in the other time zone.

33

Automatically Move the Mouse to the Default Button

You can negotiate many dialog boxes much more quickly by customizing Windows Vista to move the mouse pointer over the default dialog box button automatically.

Most dialog boxes define a *default button*, which is most often the button that dismisses the dialog box and puts the dialog box settings into effect. The most common default dialog box button is the OK button.

Many dialog boxes do nothing more than provide you with information or a warning. In most of these cases, the only thing you need to do with the dialog box is click the default button. You can get past such dialog boxes much more quickly if you customize Windows Vista to move the mouse pointer over the default button automatically.

---

① Click Start.

② Click Control Panel.

The Control Panel window appears.

③ Click Mouse.

The Mouse Properties dialog box appears.

④ Click the Pointer Options tab.

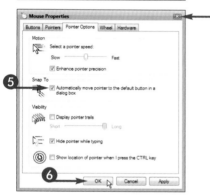

⑤ Click the Automatically move pointer to the default button in a dialog box check box (☐ changes to ☑).

⑥ Click OK.

Windows Vista automatically moves the mouse pointer to the default button each time you open a dialog box.

⑦ Click the Close box to close the Control Panel window.

Caution!

When the Snap To feature is activated, it is easy to get into the habit of quickly clicking whenever a notification dialog box appears. However, if you click too quickly, you may miss the message in the dialog box, which could be important. Remember to read all dialog box messages before clicking the default button.

You can give yourself more vertical room on your screen by hiding the Windows Vista taskbar.

As you work with Windows Vista, you may find yourself wishing you had more room on your screen to display your programs. This is particularly true for people who do a lot of writing on their computer, because they often would like to see more of their text on the screen.

Unfortunately, the Windows Vista taskbar takes up room on the bottom of the screen. Even when you maximize a program, the taskbar remains visible. However, if you do not use the taskbar to switch programs, you may no longer require the taskbar to be visible at all times, so you can configure Windows Vista to hide it and get more screen space.

① Right-click an empty section of the taskbar.

② Click Properties.

The Taskbar and Start Menu Properties dialog box appears.

③ Click the Taskbar tab.

④ Click the Auto-hide the taskbar check box (☐ changes to ☑).

⑤ Click OK.

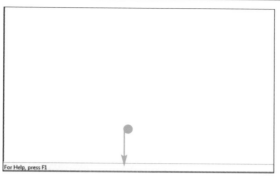

● Windows Vista hides all but a small strip of the taskbar.

For Help, press F1

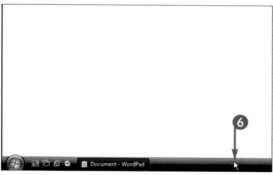

⑥ To view and work with the taskbar, move the mouse pointer to the bottom of the screen.

Document - WordPad

⑥

More Options!
If you do not want to see the taskbar at all, follow steps **1** to **3**, click to uncheck the Keep the taskbar on top of other windows check box (☑ changes to ☐), and then click OK. Note that after you do this, the only way to display the taskbar is to press the Windows Logo key or Ctrl+Esc.

Run a Program in Compatibility Mode

If you are having trouble running an older program, you can customize the program's icon to run in compatibility mode so that it will work properly under Windows Vista.

In most cases, older programs should run without any problems under Windows Vista. However, in some cases these older programs fail to run or experience problems in Windows Vista.

The most common reason for such problems is that the older program was designed specifically to run under a particular operating system. You can usually work around such problems by running the program in *compatibility mode*, where Windows Vista sets up an environment that mimics the operating system for which the program was designed.

---

① Click Start.

② Click All Programs.

③ Click the menu that contains the icon of the program you want to configure.

④ Right-click the icon.

⑤ Click Properties.

The program's Properties dialog box appears.

6 Click the Compatibility tab.

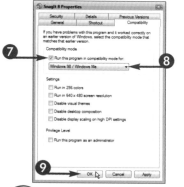

7 Click the Run this program in compatibility mode for check box (☐ changes to ☑).

8 Click here and select the operating system for which the program was designed.

9 Click OK.

Windows Vista runs the program in compatibility mode each time you start it.

Note: *If you have an older program that requires elevated privileges, see "Run a Program with Elevated Privileges" in Chapter 1.*

More Options!

Some older programs do not run under Windows Vista because they require fewer colors than Windows Vista displays. For example, many older programs can use at most 256 colors, but the Windows Vista minimum is 65,536 colors. To fix this, follow steps **1** to **6** and then click the Run in 256 colors check box (☐ changes to ☑). If your program fails because it expects a screen resolution of 640x480, click the Run in 640 x 480 screen resolution check box (☐ changes to ☑). Click OK.

You can customize Windows Vista to perform a specific action whenever you insert a particular type of media, such as an audio CD.

When you insert some types of media into your computer, you usually see a dialog box that gives you a list of actions you can perform on that media. For example, if you insert an audio CD, you have the choice of playing the CD in Windows

Media Player, ripping the songs from the CD to Windows Media Player, and so on. This is called AutoPlay and it works for the various media types, including audio CDs, DVD movies, pictures, and audio files. If you always select the same action for a particular media type, you can bypass the AutoPlay dialog box and have Windows Vista perform that action automatically.

① Click Start.

② Click Control Panel.

The Control Panel window appears.

③ Click Hardware and Sound.

The Hardware and Sound window appears.

④ Click AutoPlay.

The AutoPlay window appears.

⑤ For the media type you want to configure, click here and select the default action that you want Windows Vista to perform when you insert the media.

⑥ Repeat step **5** for the other media you want to configure.

⑦ Click Save.

⑧ Click the Close box to close Control Panel.

Windows Vista performs the default actions you chose whenever you insert the configured media.

Reverse It!

If you do not like the default action you have chosen for a media type, follow steps **1** to **4** to display the AutoPlay window. Click the down arrow (▼) for the media type, and then click Ask me every time. If you prefer to reset all the media, scroll down to the bottom of the AutoPlay window and then click Reset all defaults. Click Save.

Change a Disk's Drive Letter

You can tell Windows Vista to use a different letter for a disk drive on your system, which often makes it easier to work with your drives.

The disk drives on your computer are each assigned a letter. On most systems, the floppy drive is usually drive A and the main hard drive is usually drive C. Drives D, E, F, and so on are assigned to other

hard drives, as well as CD and DVD drives, depending on the system's configuration. In addition, if you insert a removable media, Windows Vista assigns the first available letter to the drive.

There may be times when the letters that Windows Vista assigns are not suitable. Windows Vista enables you to change the letter that is associated with a disk drive.

---

① Click Start.

② Right-click Computer.

③ Click Manage.

Note: If the User Account Control dialog box appears, click Continue or type an administrator password and click Submit.

The Computer Management window appears.

④ Click Disk Management.

⑤ Right-click the drive with which you want to work.

⑥ Click Change Drive Letter and Paths.

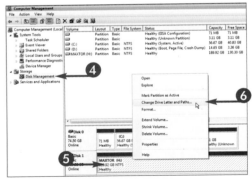

The Change Drive Letters and Paths dialog box appears.

7 Click Change.

The Change Drive Letter or Path dialog box appears.

8 Click here and select the new drive letter.

9 Click OK.

Windows Vista asks you to confirm the change.

10 Click Yes.

● Windows Vista changes the drive letter.

11 Click the Close box to close the Computer Management window.

Windows Vista uses the new letter for the disk drive.

Caution!

If you are going to change the drive letter for a hard drive, be sure to make the change before you install any programs on the drive. Otherwise, changing the drive letter will likely cause those programs to stop working and you would need to uninstall and then reinstall the programs.

Enrich Your Media Experience

Windows Vista was designed from the ground up to offer you a rich media experience. Whether you are dealing with drawings, photos, sounds, audio CDs, downloaded music files, or DVDs, the tools that are built-in to Windows Vista enable you to play, edit, and even create media.

The downside to having a rich media environment readily available is that the media tools themselves are necessarily feature-laden and complex. The basic operations are usually easy enough to master, but some of the more useful and interesting features tend to be in hard-to-find places. This chapter helps you take advantage of many of these

off-the-beaten-track features by showing you how to find and use them.

For example, you discover many useful image tips and tricks, including how to rotate an image, repair image defects such as incorrect exposure and red eye, add tags to help you categorize and find your images, and create custom file names for imported images.

On the audio front, you figure out how to adjust the settings Windows Media Player uses to rip audio tracks from a CD, how to share you media library with other people on your network, and how to set up an automatic playlist.

Quick Tips

You can ensure that the subject of an image is right-side up by rotating the image clockwise or counterclockwise as needed.

When you take a vertical shot with your digital camera, your photo appears sideways when you download the image to your computer. Windows Vista often detects photos with an incorrect rotation and asks if you want the rotation

corrected during the download. If you elected not to have the rotation fixed, you can still repair the rotation yourself.

Rotation problems are also common with scanned images, because often the only way some images will fit on the scanner bed it to place them sideways. Windows Vista does not offer to correct such images during scanning, so you need to repair the rotation yourself.

---

① Click **Start**.

② Click **All Programs**.

Note: *After you click All Programs, the name changes to Back..*

③ Click **Windows Photo Gallery**.

Windows Photo Gallery appears.

④ Click the image you want to rotate.

5 Click this button to rotate the image counterclockwise.

● If you prefer to rotate the image clockwise, click this button, instead.

You can also rotate the image by right-clicking it and then clicking either Rotate Counterclockwise or Rotate Clockwise.

Note: Press Ctrl+, to rotate the image counterclockwise; press Ctrl+. (period) to rotate the image clockwise.

● Windows Photo Gallery rotates the image.

6 Repeat steps **4** and **5** to rotate any other images that require adjusting.

7 Click the Close box to close Windows Photo Gallery.

More Options!

If you do not want Windows Photo Gallery to rotate images as you import them from your digital camera, you can turn this feature off. Click File and then click Options to display the Windows Photo Gallery Options dialog box. Click the Import tab and then click to uncheck the Rotate pictures on import check box (☑ changes to ☐). Click OK.

You can use the Windows Vista new Photo Gallery to improve the look of digital photos and other images. The Photo Gallery includes a special Fix window that offers a number of tools to repair various image attributes.

For the exposure, Photo Gallery can adjust the brightness of the image and the image contrast, which is the relative difference between the lightest and darkest areas in the image.

For the color, Photo Gallery can adjust the color temperature (the relative warmth of the colors, where cooler means bluer and hotter means redder), the tint, and the saturation (the percentage of hue in each color).

Photo Gallery also enables you to crop an image to remove unwanted subjects or to ensure that the main subject is centered in the photo.

① Click Start.

② Click All Programs.

③ Click Windows Photo Gallery.

Windows Photo Gallery appears.

④ Click the image you want to repair.

⑤ Click Fix.

The Fix window appears.

⑥ To change the exposure, click Adjust Exposure and then click and drag the Brightness and Contrast sliders.

⑦ To change the color, click Adjust Color and then click and drag the Color Temperature, Tint, and Saturation sliders.

● If you are not sure how to use these tools, click Auto Adjust to have Photo Gallery make the adjustments for you.

⑧ To remove red eye from a photo, click Fix Red Eye.

⑨ To crop the picture, first click Crop Picture.

⑩ Click here and then click the dimensions you want.

⑪ Click and drag the handles to set the new size of the image.

⑫ Click Apply.

⑬ When you are done, click Back to Gallery.

Photo Gallery applies the repairs.

Reverse It!

The Photo Gallery always keeps a backup copy of the original image, just in case. To undo all your changes and get the original image back, click the image and then click Fix. In the Fix window, click Revert and then click Revert to Original (or press Ctrl+R). When Windows Photo Gallery asks you to confirm, click Revert.

If you have images that are related in some way, you can work with them efficiently by storing them in the same folder. However, this is not always convenient. For example, if you went on trips to France, Germany, and Italy, it makes sense to store the trip photos in three separate folders. However, if you need to work with all those photos — for example, to create a DVD of your European photos — having them in separate folders is inconvenient.

The solution is to use the Windows Photo Gallery tag feature. A *tag* is a keyword that describes an image. In the previous example, you could apply the keyword Europe to all of the photos from France, Germany, and Italy.

APPLY TAGS TO IMAGES

1 Click Start.

2 Click All Programs.

3 Click Windows Photo Gallery.

Windows Photo Gallery appears.

4 Click Info.

The Info pane appears.

5 Click the image with which you want to work.

6 Click Add Tags.

- A text box appears.

7 Type a tag and press Enter.

- Tags you have added appear here.

8 Repeat steps **5** and **6** to add more tags to the image.

9 Repeat steps **4** to **8** to add tags to other images.

10 Click the Hide Info Pane button.

The Info pane disappears.

USE A TAG TO FILTER IMAGES

1 Click Tags.

2 Click the tag.

- Windows Photo Gallery displays only the images that have the selected tag applied.

TIP

More Options!
If you create a tag that you do not like or that is not descriptive enough, you can rename it to something better. Click Tags to display the list of tags, right-click the tag you want to change, and then click Rename. Type the new tag text and press Enter.

You can create more meaningful file names for your imported images by configuring Windows Photo Gallery to use a custom name that you specify during each import operation.

Most digital cameras and scanners supply images with cryptic file names, such as IMG_1083 and scan001. When you import images, these non-descriptive names can make it more difficult to find and work with images.

To work around this problem, you can configure the Windows Picture and Video Import tool to apply a custom name to your imported images. This custom name is based on a word or short phrase that you specify during the import. For example, if you specify Vacation as the event tag, then your imported images will be named Vacation 001, Vacation 002, and so on.

① Click Start.

② Click All Programs.

③ Click Windows Photo Gallery.

Windows Photo Gallery appears.

④ Click File.

⑤ Click Options.

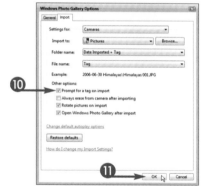

The Windows Photo Gallery Options dialog box appears.

⑥ Click the Import tab.

⑦ In the Settings for list, click here and then click the type of device with which you want to work.

⑧ In the File name list, click here and then click Tag.

⑨ Repeat steps **7** and **8** to apply the event tag filename to imports from other devices.

⑩ Click the Prompt for a tag on import check box (☐ changes to ☑).

⑪ Click OK.

Windows Photo Gallery puts the new settings into effect.

More Options!

If you always clear the memory card in your digital camera after you import the images, you can have the Windows Picture and Video Import tool do this for you automatically. In the Import tab, click the Always erase from camera after importing check box (☐ changes to ☑).

If you have a portable media device that is compatible with Windows Media Player, you synchronize that device with Media Player to ensure the device always has the music you want.

Windows Media Player supports a wide range of portable media devices. These devices include MP3 players, memory cards, digital audio receivers, network media players, and portable media centers.

When you insert a Media Player–compatible device, Media Player recognizes the device and automatically displays the device, its total capacity, and its available space in the Media Player Sync tab.

You can then specify a sync list of music files on your computer. Media Player can add those files to the device, and then keep your computer and the device synchronized as the sync list changes.

① Attach the media device to your computer.

② Click Start.

③ Click All Programs.

④ Click Windows Media Player.

Windows Media Player appears.

⑤ Click the Sync tab.

- Information about the device appears here.

6️⃣ Click and drag music from your library and drop it inside the Sync List.

- Media Player updates the space remaining on the device.

7️⃣ Click Start Sync.

Media Player adds the music to the device.

Check It Out!

If you are not sure whether a device you have is compatible with Media Player, or if you are thinking of purchasing a media device and want to ensure it is Media Player–compatible, look for the Plays for Sure logo on the box. If you are still not sure, you can search for the device at the Plays for Sure Web site at www.playsforsure.com.

Create an Automatic Playlist

You can create a playlist that Media Player maintains automatically based on the criteria you specify.

You can create a playlist based on the properties that Media Player maintains for each file. These properties include Album Artist, Genre, Composer, Rating, and so on. Therefore, you could create a playlist that includes every music file where the Genre property equals Classical.

You create a property-based playlist by specifying the playlist *criteria*, which consist of three factors: the property, the property value, and an operator that relates the two. The most common operators are Is, Is Not, and Contains.

Property-based playlists are automatic. This means that after you set up the playlist, Media Player automatically populates the playlist with all the music files that meet your criteria.

① In Windows Media Player, click the arrow below the Library tab.

② Click Create Auto Playlist.

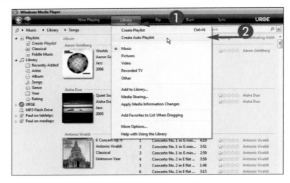

The New Auto Playlist dialog box appears.

③ Type a name for the playlist.

④ Click here to display the menu of properties.

⑤ Click a property.

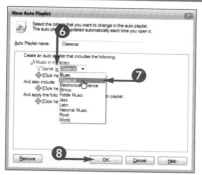

6 Click here to choose an operator.

7 Click here and then click the criteria you want to use.

8 Click OK.

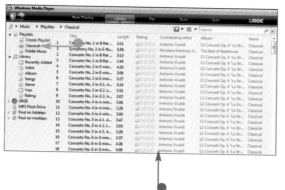

● Media Player adds your playlist to My Playlists.

● Media Player populates the playlist based on your criteria.

More Options!

You can place restrictions on your automatic playlists so that they do not become too large. Open the Playlists branch, right-click your automatic playlist, and then click Edit to display the Edit Auto Playlist dialog box. Pull down the list named And apply the following restrictions to the auto playlist, and then click Limit Number of Items, Limit Total Duration To, or Limit Total Size To. Fill in the limit, and then click OK.

Windows Media Player gives you lots of control over the copying — or *ripping* — of tracks from an audio CD by enabling you to select a format and a bit rate.

The *format* is the audio file type you want to use to store the ripped tracks on your computer. You have six choices: Windows Media Audio, Windows Media Audio Pro, Windows Media Audio (Variable Bit Rate), Windows Media Audio Lossless, MP3, and WAV.

The *bit rate* determines the quality of the rip and is measured in kilobits per second (Kbps). The higher the bit rate, the better the quality, but the more hard drive space each track uses.

① In Windows Media Player, click the arrow below the Rip tab.

② Click Format.

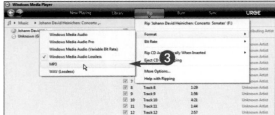

Windows Media Player displays the available audio file formats.

③ Click the format you want to use.

④ Click the arrow below the Rip tab.

⑤ Click Bit Rate.

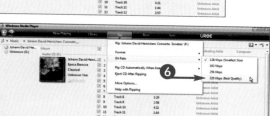

Windows Media Player displays the available bit rates.

Note: The available bit rates depend on the audio file format you chose in step 3. Note that some formats use a fixed bit rate that you cannot change.

⑥ Click the bit rate you want to use.

Windows Media Player uses the selected format and bit rate the next time you rip tracks from an audio CD.

Did You Know?

Bit Rates and Drive Space for the WMA Format

Bit Rate (Kbps)	KB/Minute	MB/Hour
48	360	21
64	480	28
96	720	42
128	960	56
160	1,200	70
192	1,440	84

You can see just the information you want for every media file by customizing the Media Player view to show the specific media details you prefer.

Windows Media Player keeps track of a great deal of information for all your media files. For music files, Media Player keeps tracks of standard properties, such as the album title, artist, and track names and lengths. However, Media Player also stores more detailed information, such as the genre, release date, bit rate, file format, and size.

These properties are called *metadata*, because they are all data that describe the media. You can customize any of the Media Player folders to display the Details view, which shows the metadata.

① Click here to open the View Options menu.

② Click Details.

● Media Player switches to Details view.

③ Click here to open the Layout Options menu.

④ Click Choose Columns.

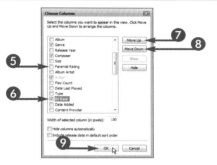

The Choose Columns dialog box appears.

5 Click the deactivated check boxes of the columns you want to view (□ changes to ☑).

6 Click to uncheck the activated check boxes of the columns you do not want to view (☑ changes to □).

7 To move the selected column to the left in Details view, click Move Up.

8 To move the selected column to the right in Details view, click Move Down.

9 Click OK.

● Media Player updates the view to display the columns you selected.

More Options!
You can see more columns in Details view if you reduce the width of each column so that it is just wide enough to display its data. The easiest way to do this is to move the mouse pointer over the right edge of the column's header — the pointer changes to a two-headed arrow with a vertical bar through it — and then double-click.

You can listen to the songs and view the photos and videos in your Media Player Library on another device by sharing your Library over a wired or wireless network.

If you have a wired or wireless network, however, you can take advantage of the Library work you have done on one computer by sharing that Library over the network. This enables any other computer using Windows Vista to include your

media in that machine's Media Player Library. This also applies to other user accounts on your computer. Those users can log on and then access your shared Library.

Your shared Library is also available to other media devices on the network, such as an Xbox 360 or a networked digital media receiver.

① In Windows Media Player, click the arrow below the Library tab.

② Click Media Sharing.

The Media Sharing dialog box appears.

③ Click the Share my media to check box (☐ changes to ☑).

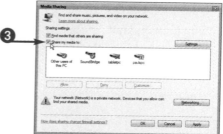

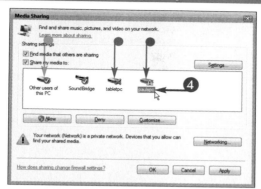

Media Player displays icons for each device to which you can share your media.

● Approved for sharing.

● Denied sharing.

● Not yet configured.

④ Click the device you want to work with.

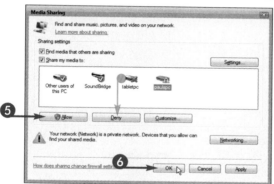

⑤ Click Allow.

● If you do not want to share your media with a device, click Deny, instead.

Note: If the User Account Control dialog box appears, click Continue or type an administrator password and click Submit.

⑥ Click OK.

Media Player shares your media on the network.

More Options!

If you want to restrict the media that you share, open the Media Sharing dialog box and click Settings to open the Default Settings dialog box. In the Media types group, click the check boxes of the media types you do not want to share (✓ changes to ☐). You can also restrict the media based on the ratings and on parental rating. Click OK to put the settings into effect.

You can control the playback of Windows Media Player, without leaving your current program, by activating and using the Media Player's toolbar.

Using Windows Media Player to play music in the background works well except when you want to make playback adjustments, such as skipping a track, changing the volume, or pausing the media while you take a phone call. You must switch from your current program to Windows Media Player, make the adjustments, and then return to your work.

Instead of switching to Windows Media Player and then back again, you can display the program's taskbar toolbar — a feature called *mini-mode*. This toolbar appears on the Windows Vista taskbar and enables you to pause playback, skip tracks, and mute or change the volume.

1 Click the Minimize button.

Windows Vista asks if you want the Windows Media Player toolbar on your taskbar.

2 Click Yes.

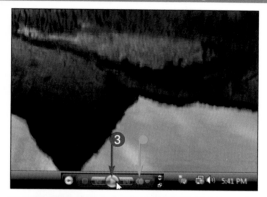

The Windows Media Player toolbar appears in place of the Windows Media Player taskbar button.

Note: *The Windows Media Player toolbar now appears each time you minimize the program. You do not need to repeat this step in the future.*

③ Click Play to begin playback of the currently selected media.

● You can click the Volume button to adjust the playback volume.

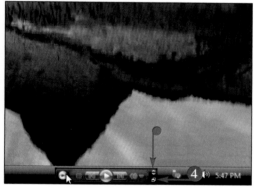

● You can click the Show Video and Visualization window button to show or hide the Video and Visualization window.

Note: *The Video and Visualization window shows the current visualization (if music is playing) or the current video. The window appears on top of any other window on your screen.*

④ Click the Restore button to restore the Windows Media Player window.

The Windows Media Player reappears.

Did You Know?

The Mini Player toolbar's Restore button (⬜) is a tiny target that is difficult to click with the mouse. To bypass the mouse and restore Windows Media Player via the keyboard, press Alt+Shift+P.

4

Get the Most Out of Your Files and Folders

Although you may use Windows Vista to achieve certain ends — write memos and letters, create presentations, play games, surf the Internet, and so on — you still have to deal with files and folders as part of your day-to-day work or play. Basic tasks such as copying and moving files, creating and renaming folders, and deleting unneeded files and folders are part of the Windows Vista routine.

Your goal should be to make all this file and folder maintenance *less* of a routine so that you have more time during the day to devote to more worthy pursuits.

Fortunately, Windows Vista offers a number of shortcuts and tweaks that can shorten file and folder tasks. In this chapter, you learn a number of these techniques.

For example, you learn how to open folders and launch files with a single-click of the mouse. You learn how to open a file in a program other than the one with which it is associated. You also learn how to perform an advanced search; how to sort, filter, group, and stack files to make them easier to find; and how to revert to a previous version of a file.

Quick Tips

Open Your Files and Folders with a Single Click

You can open files and folders more quickly by customizing Windows Vista to open items with a single mouse click instead of a double-click.

Double-clicking is not a difficult skill to learn, but it can be hard to master. For example, if you wait too long between clicks or if you move the mouse pointer slightly between the first and second click, Windows Vista interprets your action as two single-clicks instead of a double-click.

This can really slow you down. Opening files and folders with a single-click is not only faster but also more efficient. This has the added advantage of making Windows Vista more consistent; for example, you already open items on the Start menu with a single-click.

❶ In any folder window, click the Organize list's menu.

❷ Click Folder and Search Options.

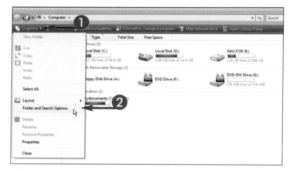

The Folder Options dialog box appears.

❸ Click the General tab.

❹ Click the Single-click to open an item (point to select) option (◯ changes to ◉).

5 Click OK.

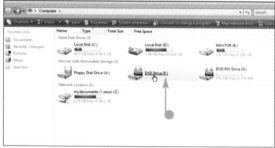

● When you hover the mouse pointer over a file or folder, Windows Vista places an underline under the icon label to remind you to use a single-click.

Note: With single-clicking activated, you select a file or folder by pointing at it with your mouse pointer.

More Options!

To make it easier to remember to single-click, you can configure Windows Vista to underline *all* your files and folders. Follow steps **1** to **4** in this task and then click the Underline icon titles consistent with my browser option (○ changes to ◉). Click OK to put the new setting into effect. If you think the underlines make your folders look cluttered, follow steps **1** to **4** and click the Underline icon titles only when I point at them option (○ changes to ◉).

Open a File with a Different Program

You can open a file in a different program from the one that is normally associated with the file. This enables you to use the other program's features to work on the file.

Every document you create has a particular file type. *File types* are Text Documents, Rich Text Documents, Bitmap Images, JPEG Images, and more. All these types have a default program associated with them.

You may have situations where you prefer to open a particular file with a different program. For example, double-clicking a picture file opens in the Photo Gallery Viewer. However, you may prefer to open the picture file in Paint or some other image-editing program so that you can make changes to the picture.

---

① **Open the folder that contains the file you want to open.**

② **Click the file.**

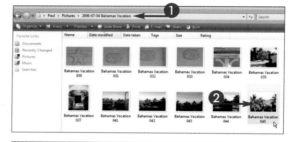

③ **Click the Preview menu.**

● **If the program you want to use appears here, click the program, and skip the remaining steps.**

④ **Click Choose Default Program.**

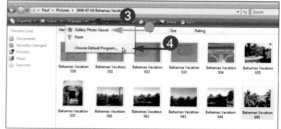

The Open With dialog box appears.

⑤ If you do not see a list of programs, double-click Other Programs.

⑥ Click the program you want to use to open the file.

● If the program you want to use does not appear in the list, you can click Browse and use the new Open With dialog box to specify the program.

⑦ Click to uncheck the Always use the selected program to open this kind of file check box (☑ changes to ☐).

⑧ Click OK.

Windows Vista opens the file in the program you chose.

More Options!
Besides opening the file you selected in the new program, you may prefer to open every other file of the same type — such as Text documents or Rich Text Format documents — in the same program. Follow steps **1** to **5** and then click the Always use the selected program to open this kind of file check box (☐ changes to ☑).

You can enhance the value of the Send To menu, making copying files and folders faster, by customizing the menu with your own destinations.

After you right-click a file or folder, you can then click Send To to reveal the Windows Vista Send To menu. This handy menu offers a number of destinations, depending on your computer's configuration: Compressed (zipped) Folder, Desktop (create

shortcut), Documents, Fax Recipient, and Mail Recipient. You may also see other removable disk drives, such as a recordable CD drive. When you click one of these destinations, Windows Vista sends a copy of the selected file or folder to that location.

To make a good thing even better, you can add your own destinations to the Send To menu.

---

① Press Windows Logo+R.

The Run dialog box appears.

② Type **%userprofile%\ appdata\Roaming \Microsoft\Windows\ SendTo**.

③ Click OK.

The SendTo window appears.

● The window shows all the items in the Send To menu, except for your floppy and removable drives.

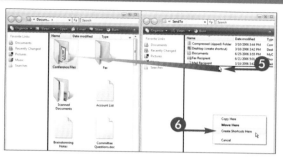

④ Open the folder containing the destination you want to add to the Send To menu.

This example uses Conference Files as the destination folder.

⑤ Right-click and drag the destination item and drop it in the SendTo window.

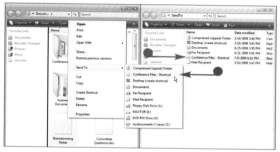

⑥ Click Create Shortcuts Here from the menu that appears after you drop the item.

● Windows Vista adds a shortcut for the destination in the SendTo window.

● The destination now appears in the Send To menu. To view it, you can click any file or folder, File, and then Send To.

Customize It!

You can customize the Send To menu with more than just folders. For example, if your system has multiple printers, you can add them to the Send To menu and then easily send a document to any printer. To add a printer to the Send To menu, click Start and then Control Panel. In the Control Panel window, click Printers. Click and drag the printer to drop it in the SendTo window.

You can prevent other people from making changes to an important file by designating the file as read-only.

Occasionally you may create or work with a file that is important. It could be a carefully crafted letter or a memo detailing important company strategy. Whatever the content, such a file requires extra protection to ensure that you do not lose your work.

You can set advanced file permissions that can prevent a document from being changed or even deleted (see "Protect a File or Folder with Permission" in Chapter 8). If your only concern is preventing other people from making changes to a document, a simpler technique you can use is making the document *read-only*.

MAKE A FILE
READ-ONLY

① Open the folder that contains the file with which you want to work.

② Right-click the file.

③ Click Properties.

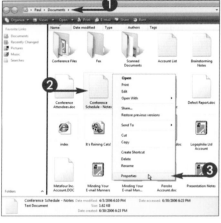

The file's Properties dialog box appears.

④ Click the General tab.

⑤ Click the Read-only check box (☐ changes to ☑).

⑥ Click OK.

The file is now read-only.

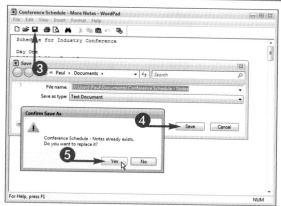

CONFIRM THAT A FILE IS READ-ONLY

1️⃣ Double-click a read-only file to open it.

2️⃣ Make changes to the file.

3️⃣ Click the Save button.

The Save As dialog box appears.

4️⃣ Click Save.

5️⃣ Click Yes.

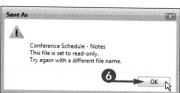

The program tells you it cannot create (save) the file, confirming that the file is read-only.

6️⃣ Click OK.

More Options!

You can hide a file that contains sensitive data to prevent other people from viewing. Follow steps **1** to **4**. Click the Hidden check box (☐ changes to ☑), click OK, and then press F5. The file icon disappears.

Perform an Advanced File Search

You can take advantage of the many new file properties supported by Windows Vista to search for files based on the author, keywords, and other data.

In Windows Vista, however, you can perform sophisticated searches by using a number of different properties, including some of the new file properties supported by Vista. These file properties are called *metadata*, because they are data that describes the data on your system — that is, your documents.

Windows Vista also supports advanced searches for particular types of files, including e-mail messages, documents, pictures, and music. For music files, you can search on the Title, Artists, and Album properties. For e-mail, you can search on the Subject, From names, and To names.

PERFORM AN ADVANCED SEARCH USING PROPERTIES

① Open the folder in which you want to search.

Note: *If you want to search all your documents, click Start, click Search, and then skip to step 5.*

② Click the Organize menu.

③ Click Layout.

④ Click Search Pane.

● The Search Pane appears.

⑤ To search for a particular type of file, click a Show only button.

⑥ Click Advanced Search.

The Advanced Search options appear.

The fields you see in this screen depend on the type of document you selected in step **5**.

7 Fill in the property values of the documents you want to find.

8 Click Search.

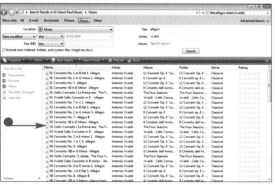

● Windows Vista displays the files that match your search criteria.

More Options!

When you type a value in a property text box, Windows Vista matches those files where the value is a partial match. For example, if you type allegro in the Title property, Windows Vista matches every music file that contains the word *allegro*. If you prefer exact matches, click Organize and then Folder and Search Options. Click the Search tab and then click to deactivate the Find partial matches check box (☐ changes to ☑). Click OK.

Windows Vista enables you to search using three different date types: Date modified, which is the date you last changed the file; Date created, which is the date you originally created the file; and Date accessed, which is the last time you opened the file. In each case, you can also choose one of three date operators:

Is, which matches a specific date; Is before, which matches all dates before the one you specify; and Is after, which matches all dates after the one you specify.

You can also search for documents based on their size using one of three operators: Equals, Is less than, or Is greater than. You then specify a size in kilobytes.

PERFORM AN ADVANCED SEARCH BY DATE

① Follow steps **1** to **6** on the previous pages to display the Advanced Search options.

② Click here and then click the type of date you want to search.

③ Click here to select the date operator you want to use.

④ Click here to select the calendar date you want to use.

⑤ Click Search.

Windows Vista displays the files that match your search criteria.

PERFORM AN ADVANCED SEARCH BY SIZE

1 Follow steps **1** to **6** on the previous pages to display the Advanced Search options.

2 Click here to select the size operator you want to use.

3 Type a size in kilobytes.

4 Click Search.

Windows Vista displays the files that match your search criteria.

Note: To learn how to improve search performance by adding folders to the Windows Vista search index, see "Search Files Faster by Adding a Folder to the Index" in Chapter 1.

Note: To learn how to save your search details and reuse them later on, see "Save Time by Saving and Reusing a Search."

Did You Know?
After you run the search, you can perform another search quickly by choosing a different operator. Pull down the list of operators, click the operator you want, and then click Search. Windows Vista runs the new search.

Save Time by Saving and Reusing a Search

You can set up and run an advanced search using the Windows Vista search engine (see "Perform an Advanced File Search"). This is a powerful tool for finding files on your system, but setting up a search can be time-consuming — particularly one that uses multiple search filters. If there are searches that you plan on running regularly, it is inefficient to have to set up the same search criteria over and over.

The solution to this problem is to save your search as one of the Windows Vista new search folders. A *search folder* is a collection of files and folders from your system that match a specified set of search criteria.

SAVE A SEARCH

① Set up and run an advanced search.

Note: *See "Perform an Advanced File Search" to learn how to create an advanced search.*

② Click Search.

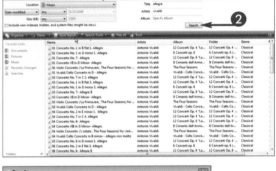

The Save As dialog box appears.

③ Type a file name for the search folder.

④ Type one or more tags (this is optional).

⑤ Click Save.

Windows Vista saves the search as a search folder.

REUSE A SEARCH

① In any folder window, click Searches.

The Saved Searches folder appears.

This folder displays the search folders saved on your system.

② Double-click the search folder you want to open.

Windows Vista runs the search and displays the results.

Did You Know?

Windows Vista comes with six predefined search folders, including five that show you recent activity on your computer: Recent Documents, Recent E-mail, Recent Music, Recent Pictures and Videos, and Recently Changed. There is also a Shared By Me search that shows the folders and files you are sharing with other users.

Find Files Faster by Sorting and Filtering

You can find the files in a folder faster by sorting the files based on the values in a property, or by filtering the folder to show only files that have a certain property value.

You can use file metadata (see "Perform an Advanced File Search") to organize a folder in a way that makes it easier to find the file or files with which you want to work. One way to organize a folder is to sort the files based on the values in a particular file property.

Another way to organize a folder is to *filter* the files based on the unique values in a particular file property. This means that you configure the folder to display only those files that have a particular value in that property.

SORTING FILES

① Open the folder you want to sort.

② Click the column menu you want to use for the sort.

③ Click Sort.

④ Repeat steps **2** and **3** to switch the sort order between ascending and descending.

Windows Vista sorts the files based on the field.

● This arrow tells you which column is being used to sort the files, and it tells you the direction of the sort (up for ascending; down for descending).

Note: *A quick way to sort the files in a folder is to click the header of the column on which you want to sort the files. Click the header again to switch the sort order.*

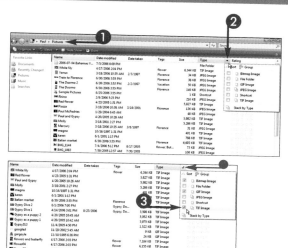

FILTERING FILES

1 Open the folder you want to filter.

2 Click a column's menu to display a list of the unique values in the column.

Note: For some columns, Windows Vista displays a range of values instead of specific values. For date-related columns, you also see a calendar that enables you to filter based on a specific date.

3 Click the check box for each value you want to include (☐ changes to ☑).

● Windows Vista filters the files to show just those that have the property value that matches one of the activated check boxes.

● A check mark appears here to indicate that you have applied a filter to the column.

Customize It!

If you want to sort or filter the folder using a field that is not displayed, right-click any column header and then click the name of the column you want to use. Click More to see a full list of the available columns.

Organize Files by Grouping and Stacking

You can make the files in a folder easier to manage and work with by organizing them into groups and stacks.

Grouping files means organizing them into distinct categories based on the property values in a particular column. For example, if you group a folder based on the Type column, Windows Vista displays files of the same type together in a group. You

can then work with that group as a whole — move it, delete it, and so on.

Stacking files also means organizing them based on the unique property values in a particular column. However, each stack is a kind of virtual folder that holds the files that share a particular property value.

GROUP FILES

① Open the folder you want to group.

② Click the field's menu you want to use for the grouping.

③ Click Group.

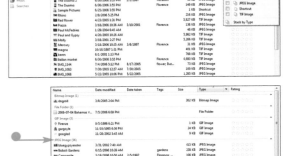

Windows Vista groups the files.

● Each group has its own header that identifies the group and tells you how many files are in the group.

STACK FILES

① Open the folder you want to group.

② Click the field's menu you want to use for the stacks.

③ Click Stack by *Field*, where *Field* is the name of the field you are using (for example, Stack by Type).

Windows Vista stacks the files.

● Each icon represents a stack.

④ Double-click a stack to open it and see its files.

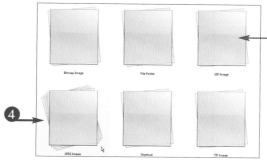

Did You Know?

When you group a folder, you can *collapse* the group — hide everything but the group header — by double-clicking the group header. To *expand* the group — display the group's files — double-click the header again. You can also click a group header to select all the files in that group, and you can click and drag the group header to move or copy the entire group to another location.

Move Your Documents Folder

By default, your Documents folder is located in C:\Users*User*\Documents, where *User* is your Windows Vista user name. However, when you use Documents in your everyday work, this location is transparent to you because Windows Vista enables you to open the folder directly.

That feature is convenient, but what if the default location of the Documents folder becomes a problem? For example, you may find that drive C is running low on hard drive space. In addition, many people add to their computer a second hard drive — usually drive D — in which to store their documents. However, having some files in Documents and others in drive D can be a hassle.

To solve both problems, you can move Documents to another location.

---

① If the folder to which you want to move Documents does not yet exist, create the folder.

② Click Start.

③ Right-click Documents.

④ Click Properties.

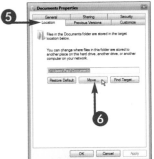

The Documents Properties dialog box appears.

⑤ Click the Location tab.

⑥ Click Move.

The Select a Destination dialog box appears.

⑦ Click the hard drive or folder that you want to use as the new location for Documents.

⑧ Click Select Folder to return to the Documents Properties dialog box.

● The new location appears in the text box.

⑨ Click OK.

Windows Vista asks you if you want to move the existing Documents folder files to the new location.

⑩ Click Yes.

Windows Vista moves the Documents folder and its files to the new location.

Apply It!
You can use the technique in this task to move any of your user folders, including Pictures, Music, Videos, Contacts, Downloads, and Favorites. Click Start and then click your user name to view all your user folders, right-click the folder you want to move, and then click Properties.

Restore a Previous Version of a File

If you improperly edit, accidentally delete, or corrupt a file through a system crash, in many cases you can restore a previous version of the file.

Each time you start your computer, Windows Vista takes a "snapshot" of its current contents. As you work on your files throughout the day, Windows Vista keeps track of the changes you make to

each file. This gives Windows Vista the capability to reverse the changes you have made to a file to revert to the version of the file that existed when Windows Vista took its system snapshot. An earlier state of a file is called a *previous version*.

---

① Open the folder that contains the file you want to restore.

② Right-click the file.

③ Click Restore previous versions.

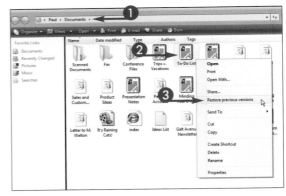

Windows Vista displays the file's Properties dialog box and the Previous Versions tab.

The File versions list shows you the previous versions of the file that exist.

④ Click a previous version.

⑤ Click Restore.

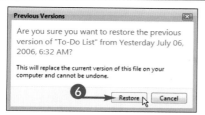

Windows Vista asks you to confirm that you want to restore the previous version.

⑥ Click Restore.

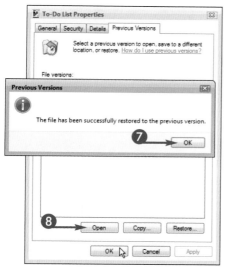

Windows Vista restores the previous version.

⑦ Click OK.

⑧ Click OK.

More Options!

If you are not sure which previous version to restore, click the previous version and then click Open to view the version. If you are still not sure, create a copy: Click the previous versions, click Copy, click a folder to store the copy, and then click Copy.

Enhance Internet Security and Privacy

The Internet is now the online home away from home for hundreds of millions of people around the world. The lure of all that information, entertainment, and camaraderie has proven to be simply impossible to resist.

But the Internet has also lured more than its fair share of another class of people: malicious hackers, system intruders, and con artists of every stripe. These miscreants seem to spend most of their waking hours thinking up new ways to disrupt the Internet, break into your online computer, and steal everything from your credit card number to your full identity. Thankfully, such as crime in the real world, online crime is still relatively rare. However, as the

newspaper headlines attest almost daily, cybercrime is a big business, and so it pays to play it safe.

This chapter helps by offering you a full suite of tasks and techniques designed to make your Internet sessions as safe as possible. You learn how to block specific Web sites; how to restrict Internet content; how to prevent a user from downloading files; how to scan your system for spyware; how to use e-mail and Web media safely and securely; and how to reduce junk e-mail.

Quick Tips

Protect Children by Activating Parental Controls

You can make computing safer for your children by activating the Windows Vista parental controls feature.

You can restrict the Web sites, games, and other content viewed by your children by activating the parental controls feature. Parental controls also enable you to set time limits on computer use and to view computer activity reports for your children.

Parental controls are also useful for keeping your computer safe from the activities of innocent or inexperienced users. For example, you can prevent children from downloading files that might contain a virus.

Note that for parental controls to work, you must set up separate user accounts for the children who use your computer. When you create these accounts, make sure you set them up as Standard user accounts.

---

① Click Start.

② Click Control Panel.

The Control Panel window appears.

③ Click Set up parental controls for any user.

Note: *If the User Account Control dialog box appears, click Continue or type an administrator password and click Submit.*

The Parental Controls window appears.

④ Click the user you want to control.

The User Controls window appears.

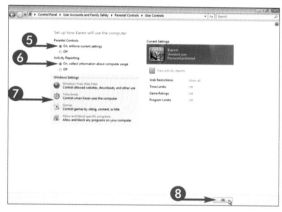

⑤ Click the On, enforce current settings option (○ changes to ◉).

The Settings links become available.

⑥ Click the On, collect information about computer usage option (○ changes to ◉).

⑦ Click the links in the Windows Settings groups to configure controls for the user.

Note: See the section "Avoid Objectionable Material by Filtering Web Content" to learn how to set up the Windows Vista Web Filter.

⑧ Click OK.

Windows Vista activates parental controls for the user.

More Options!

To restrict the times that the person can use the computer, click Time limits to display an hourly time grid. Click the hour blocks that you do not want the person to use the computer, and then click OK. To specify the programs the user can run, click Allow and block specific programs and then click the *User* can only use the programs I allow option (○ changes to ◉). Click the check boxes beside the allowed programs (☐ changes to ☑), and then click OK.

Avoid Objectionable Material by Filtering Web Content

You can block objectionable material on the Web by configuring Windows Vista to not display certain Web sites and certain types of Web content for a particular person who uses your computer.

The Web is a vast resource that has a great deal of entertaining or interesting information. However, unlike television, magazines, newspapers, and books, no one controls the content on the Web.

Therefore, there are many sites that contain objectionable content.

If you share your computer with children, you can configure the Windows Vista Web Filter to block certain Web sites that you do not want those children to view. You can also filter Web content by setting up a restriction level or by blocking specific types of Web content.

Note: *Before performing the step in this section, be sure to activate parental controls. See the section "Protect Children by Activating Parental Controls."*

① Open the User Controls window for the user you want to control.

② Click Windows Vista Web Filter.

The Web Restrictions window appears.

③ Click the Block some websites or content option (◯ changes to ◉).

④ Click Edit the Allow and block list.

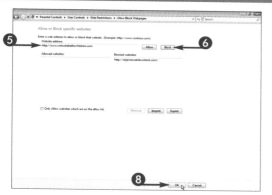

The Allow Block Webpages window appears.

5 Type the address of a site you want to block.

6 Click Block.

● Windows Vista adds the address to the Blocked websites list.

7 Repeat steps **5** and **6** to block more sites.

8 Click OK.

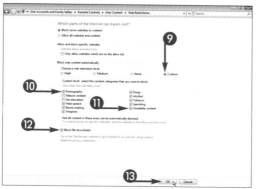

9 Click the Custom option (○ changes to ⦿).

10 Click the check box for each Web content category that you want to block (▢ changes to ☑).

11 To block unrated sites, click the Unratable content check box (▢ changes ☑).

12 To prevent the user from downloading files, click the Block file downloads check box (▢ changes ☑).

13 Click OK.

Windows Vista puts the Web restrictions into effect.

More Options!

For very young children, you may want to block off the entire Web except for sites you specify. To do this, click the Highest restriction option (○ changes to ⦿). Then click Allow or Block specific websites, and for each allowed site, type its address and click Allow.

You can ensure that your computer is free of malicious software by scanning your computer for installed spyware.

One of the most common Internet-based threats to your computer is a type of software called spyware. *Spyware* refers to a program installed on your system without your knowledge to surreptitiously monitor your computer activities — particularly the typing of sensitive data, such as passwords,

PINs, and credit card numbers — or to gather sensitive data from your computer.

Most spyware programs install themselves by being bundled together with legitimate programs that you download from the Internet. After a spyware program is on your computer, to remove it you need to use an anti-spyware program, such as Windows Defender, which comes with Windows Vista.

① Click Start.

② Click All Programs.

Note: *After you click All Programs, the name changes to Back.*

③ Click Windows Defender.

The Windows Defender window appears.

④ Click the Scan menu.

⑤ Click Full Scan.

Windows Defender begins the scan and displays the progress.

● If you need to interrupt the scan, click Stop Scan.

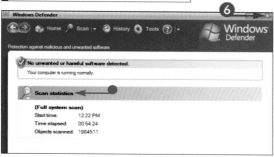

● When the scan is complete, Windows Defender displays the results.

Note: If Windows Defender finds any spyware, it displays a list of the programs. Follow the instructions on the screen to remove the spyware.

⑥ Click here to close Windows Defender.

More Options!

By default, Windows Defender performs a Quick Scan of your computer every night at 2:00 AM if your computer is turned on. To run the more comprehensive Full Scan, instead, click Tools and then click Options. In the Type list, click Full system scan and then click Save.

Play Web Page Media Safely and Privately

You can set options in Windows Media Player to ensure that media downloaded from or played on an Internet site is safe and to enhance the privacy of the Internet media you play.

When you play Internet media, the person who created the media may have included extra commands in a script that is designed to control the playback. Unfortunately, scripts can also contain commands that

can harm your computer, so preventing these scripts from running is the best option.

Also, Media Player stores the names of media files that you play and the addresses of Web sites that you visit. If other people use or have access to your computer, you may want to enhance your privacy by not allowing Media Player to store this history.

---

① In Windows Media Player, click the Library tab's menu.

② Click More Options.

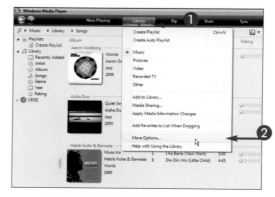

The Options dialog box appears.

③ Click the Security tab.

④ Click the Run script commands and rich media streams when the Player is in a Web page check box (☑ changes to ☐).

5 Click the Privacy tab.

6 Click the Save file and URL history in the Player check box (☑ changes to ☐).

7 Click OK.

Windows Media Player puts the new security and privacy options into effect.

Important!

Some content sites require a Player ID before you can play any media. For example, a site may request the ID for billing purposes. In that case, enable Media Player to send the ID by displaying the Privacy tab and clicking the Send unique Player ID to content providers check box (☐ changes to ☑).

Set the Junk E-Mail Protection Level to Avoid Spam

You can configure the Windows Mail junk e-mail protection level to strike a balance between avoiding spam and missing important non-spam messages.

When trying to prevent junk e-mail, your goal should be to find a protection level that flags the most spam and the fewest false positives — legitimate messages flagged as spam. To help you do this, Windows Mail offers four protection levels:

The No Automatic Filtering level turns off the junk e-mail filter. The Low level flags only messages with obvious spam content. The High level handles spam aggressively, so it almost never misses a junk e-mail, but it also generates regular false positives. The Safe Lists Only level treats all incoming messages as spam, except for messages from people in your Safe Senders list (see the section "Add a Person to Your Safe Senders List.").

---

① Click Start.

② Click E-mail.

The Windows Mail window appears.

③ Click Tools.

④ Click Junk E-mail Options.

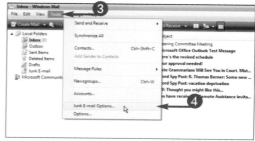

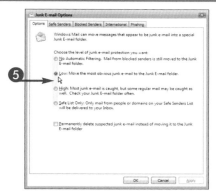

The Junk E-mail Options dialog box appears.

⑤ Click the junk e-mail protection level option that you want to use (○ changes to ◉).

⑥ Click the Phishing tab.

⑦ Click the Move phishing E-mail to the Junk Mail folder check box (☐ changes to ☑).

Note: A phishing e-mail is a message that pretends to be from a legitimate business. The message includes links for a Web site where you are asked to provide a password or other sensitive information.

⑧ Click OK.

Windows Mail puts the new settings into effect.

Reverse It!

If you select the High level of junk e-mail protection, be sure to check the Junk E-mail folder regularly to look for false positives. If you get a false positive in your Junk E-mail folder, click the message and then click Message, Junk E-mail, Mark as Not Junk. Windows Mail returns the message to the Inbox folder.

Add a Person to Your Blocked Senders List

If you receive spam or other unwanted messages from a particular person, you can configure Windows Mail to block that person's address so that you do not have to deal with that person's messages.

Sometimes a particular person sends junk messages using a legitimate return e-mail address. In this case, you can add that address to the Windows Mail Blocked Senders list. Any future messages from

that person — as well as any messages from that person currently in your Inbox folder — are automatically rerouted to the Junk E-mail folder.

However, the Blocked Senders list is not just for spam. If you have a person who is sending you annoying or offensive messages, you can add that person's address to the Blocked Senders list.

---

① In Windows Mail, click Tools.

② Click Junk E-mail Options.

Note: If you have a message from a person you want to block, click the message, click Message, click Junk E-mail, and then click Add Sender to Blocked Senders List.

The Junk E-mail Options dialog box appears.

③ Click the Blocked Senders tab.

④ Click Add.

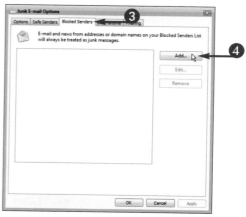

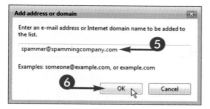

The Add address or domain dialog box appears.

⑤ Type the address of the person you want to block.

⑥ Click OK.

● Windows Mail adds the address to the Blocked Senders list.

⑦ Repeat steps **4** to **6** to add more addresses to your Blocked Senders list.

⑧ Click OK.

If any of the people you added to the Blocked Senders list have messages in your Inbox folder, Windows Mail moves those messages to the Junk E-mail folder.

Try This!

Some spammers use varying addresses that change the user name but keep the same domain name — for example, sales@spammer.com, offers@spammer.com, and so on. To block all messages from this type of spammer, add just the domain name — spammer.com in this example — to the Blocked Senders list.

Block Messages from a Country to Reduce Spam

If you receive spam from e-mail addresses that originate in a particular country, you can avoid dealing with those messages by telling Windows Mail to block messages that come from that country.

Many of the Internet domain names end with country or region codes. For example, .ca is the domain code for Canada, .uk is for Great Britain, .de is for Germany, and .us is for the United States.

If you are getting spam from addresses that use a domain code for a particular country, you can configure Windows Mail to block messages from such domains. Any future messages from that country — as well as any messages from that country currently in your Inbox folder — are automatically moved to the Junk E-mail folder.

---

① In Windows Mail, click Tools.

② Click Junk E-mail Options.

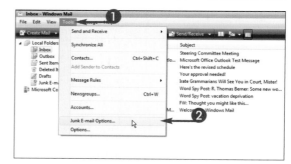

The Junk E-mail Options dialog box appears.

③ Click the International tab.

④ Click Blocked Top-Level Domain List.

The Blocked Top-Level Domain List dialog box appears.

5 Click the check box for each country you want to block (□ changes to ☑).

6 Click OK.

7 Click OK.

Windows Mail begins blocking messages from the country or countries you selected.

If any of the messages in your Inbox folder come from the blocked countries, Windows Mail moves those messages to the Junk E-mail folder.

Try This!

If you regularly get messages written in a language that you do not understand, you should treat such messages as junk e-mail. To configure Windows Mail to block such messages, follow steps **1** to **3** and then click Blocked Encoding List. In the Blocked Encoding List dialog box, click the check box for each language you want to block (□ changes to ☑), and then click OK.

Add a Person to Your Safe Senders List

If you want to receive e-mail messages from only a particular group of people, you can add those people to your Safe Senders list. Windows Mail will block all other incoming messages.

If you have set the junk e-mail protection level, blocking the addresses of known spammers, and have blocked spam that originates in some countries, then you should have your spam problem under control.

If you are still receiving too much junk e-mail, then it may be time for you to try the opposite approach. That is, you can configure Windows Mail to allow only mail from addresses that you specify — the Safe Senders list. This method virtually eliminates spam from getting to you.

① In Windows Mail, click Tools.

② Click Junk E-mail Options.

Note: If you have a message from a person you want add to your Safe Senders list, click the message, click Message, click Junk E-mail, and then click Add Sender to Safe Senders List.

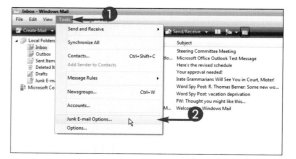

The Junk E-mail Options dialog box appears.

③ Click the Safe Senders tab.

④ Click Add.

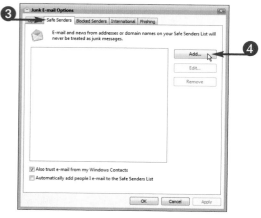

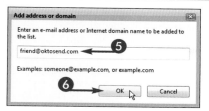

The Add address or domain dialog box appears.

⑤ Type the address of the person from whom you want to receive messages.

⑥ Click OK.

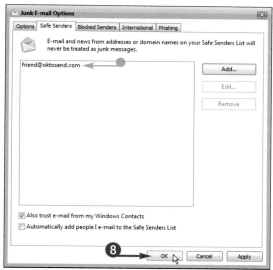

● Windows Mail adds the address to the Safe Senders list.

⑦ Repeat steps **4** to **6** to add more addresses to your Safe Senders list.

⑧ Click OK.

Try This!

If you correspond with several people who work for a particular company, you do not need to add each person's address to your Safe Senders list. Instead, you can save time by adding just the company's domain name to the Safe Senders list. That way, you see all the messages that come from that company, even from people you have never corresponded with in the past.

Prevent Windows Mail from Sending a Read Receipt

You can block Windows Mail from sending a message that confirms you have opened a message.

A *read receipt* is a short message that Windows Mail automatically fires back to the sender when you open or preview a message from that person. The read receipt — which must be requested by the sender — ensures the sender that you have viewed the message. However, many people consider this an invasion of privacy, so they block Windows Mail from sending read receipts.

By default, Windows Mail displays a dialog box that tells you the sender has requested a read receipt. You can block read receipts either by declining to send one each time Windows Mail asks or by blocking read receipts entirely.

PREVENT A SINGLE READ RECEIPT

● This dialog box appears when the sender requests a read receipt.

① Click No.

PREVENT ALL READ RECEIPTS

① In Windows Mail, click Tools.

② Click Options.

The Options dialog box appears.

③ Click the Receipts tab.

④ Click the Never send a read receipt option (○ changes to ⦿).

⑤ Click OK.

Windows Mail stops sending read receipts to confirm that you have read e-mail.

More Options!

You may find that read receipts are useful in business. For example, if someone sends you an important message, it is easier to confirm that you have received the message by having Windows Mail send a read receipt than sending a response yourself. In that case, click the Notify me for each read receipt request option (○ changes to ⦿). This enables you to control when you send a read receipt.

Configure Windows Mail to Thwart E-Mail Viruses

You can reduce the danger of accidentally unleashing a virus on your computer by reading all your e-mail messages in text format.

The HTML message format utilizes the same codes that are used to create Web pages. This means that HTML messages can use different fonts, colors, and any of the other formatting that you see on Web pages.

However, some Web pages are unsafe because they contain malicious scripts that cause problems on your computer. Unfortunately, this means HTML-formatted e-mail messages also can be unsafe because they may contain virus scripts that run automatically when you open or even just preview a message. You can prevent these scripts from running by viewing all your messages in the plain text format.

---

① In Windows Mail, click Tools.

② Click Options.

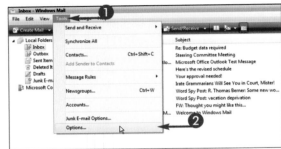

The Options dialog box appears.

③ Click the Read tab.

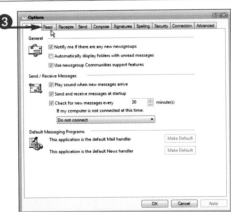

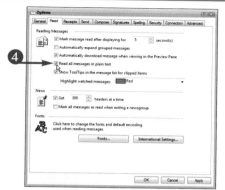

④ Click the Read all messages in plain text check box (☐ changes to ☑).

⑤ Click OK.

Windows Mail displays all messages in plain text instead of HTML.

Note: When you are viewing a message as plain text, you may realize that the message is innocuous and that it is okay to view the HTML version. To switch quickly to HTML, click View and then click Message in HTML. You can also press Alt+Shift+H.

More Options!

Windows Mail has several other options that thwart viruses. They are usually activated by default, but you should make sure of this. In the Options dialog box, click the Security tab. Click the Restricted sites zone option (○ changes to ◉), and the Warn me when other applications try to send mail as me and the Do not allow attachments to be saved or opened that could potentially be a virus check boxes (☐ changes to ☑).

Unleash the Power of Internet Explorer

The World Wide Web is arguably the most impressive of the various services accessible via the Internet. With *billions* of pages available covering practically every imaginable topic, the Web is one of our greatest inventions and an unparalleled source of information.

One problem with the Web, though, is actually getting at all that information. With so much online ground to cover, you want a reliable and efficient means of transportation. For the World Wide Web, the vehicle of choice is the Web browser, and in Windows XP, the default Web browser is Internet Explorer. This program

is easy to use if all you do is click links and type Web site addresses. However, to get the most out of the Web, you can tap into the impressive array of features and options that Internet Explorer offers.

This chapter helps you do just that by taking you through a few truly useful tips and tricks that unleash the power of Internet Explorer. You learn how to take advantage of the new tabs in the Windows Vista version of Internet Explorer; subscribe to Web feeds; use your favorite search engine with Internet Explorer; and quickly delete your browsing history.

Quick Tips

Automatically Switch to New Tabs

You can make the Internet Explorer tab feature much more convenient by configuring the program to switch to new tabs as you create them automatically.

The new version of Internet Explorer that comes with Windows Vista supports *tabbed browsing*, which means you can open multiple Web sites at once in a single browser window. Each site appears in its own tab, and you can switch from one site to another just by clicking the tabs.

To open a site in a new tab, right-click the link and then click Open in New Tab. Internet Explorer creates the tab and then opens the Web page in the tab. However, to see the page, you must then click the tab.

---

1 Click Tools.

2 Click Internet Options.

The Internet Options dialog box appears.

3 Click the General tab.

4 In the Tabs group, click Settings.

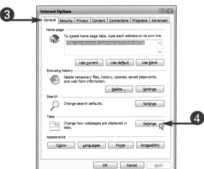

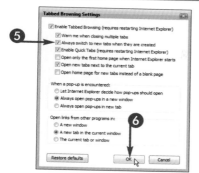

The Tabbed Browsing Settings dialog box appears.

⑤ Click the Always switch to new tabs when they are created check box (☐ changes to ✓).

⑥ Click OK.

⑦ Click OK.

More Options!

When you create a new tab by clicking the New Tab button or pressing Ctrl+T, Internet Explorer displays a blank page. To load your home page instead, follow steps **1** to **4**, click the Open home page for new tabs instead of a blank page check box (☐ changes to ✓), and then click OK.

View Open Pages as Quick Tabs

You can easily view and switch between the Web pages open in your tabs by using the Internet Explorer Quick Tabs feature.

If you have more tabs open than Internet Explorer can display, the program adds arrow buttons to scroll left and right through the tabs. However, scrolling is not always convenient because each tab gives you only a minimum amount of information.

When you are dealing with a large number of tabs, a faster way to navigate the tabs is to use the Internet Explorer Quick Tabs feature, which displays a thumbnail image of each open Web page. You can then click the thumbnail of the page you want to switch to and the tab appears immediately.

---

① Open pages in two or more tabs.

② Click the Quick Tabs button.

Note: You can also select the Quick Tabs button by pressing Ctrl+Q.

Internet Explorer displays thumbnail images of the Web pages in each tab.

③ Click the Web page you want to view.

Internet Explorer switches to the tab that contains the Web page you selected.

Remove It!

If you find that you do not use the Quick Tabs feature, you can turn it off to make room for more tabs. Click Tools and then click Internet Options to display the Internet Options dialog box. In the General tab, click Settings in the Tabs group and then click the Enable Quick Tabs check box (☑ changes to ☐). Click OK in the open dialog boxes and then restart Internet Explorer.

If you regularly view several different pages at the start of each Internet Explorer session, you can save time by opening those pages automatically each time you start Internet Explorer.

You may have more than one page that you open after Internet Explorer starts. For example, you may open a portal page such as MSN or Yahoo, a search page such as Google, your company's external or internal Web site, a news page, one or more blogger pages, and so on. Opening each new tab and navigating to the appropriate page can take time.

The Windows Vista version of Internet Explorer enables you to define multiple home pages. Internet Explorer automatically opens each home page in its own tab when you launch the program.

---

1 Open the Web page that you want to add as a home page.

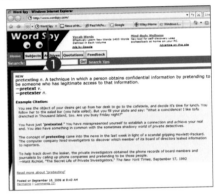

2 Click the Home menu.

3 Click Add or Change Home Page.

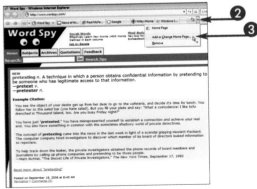

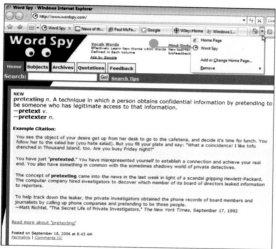

The Add or Change Home Page dialog box appears.

④ Click the Add this webpage to your home page tabs option (◯ changes to ◉).

⑤ Click Yes.

● Internet Explorer adds the page to the Home list.

Remove It!

If you have set up a site as one of your Internet Explorer home pages, but you no longer visit that site, you should remove it to reduce the time it takes for Internet Explorer to launch. Click the Home menu, click Remove, and then click the home page that you want to delete. When Internet Explorer asks you to confirm, click Yes.

You can keep up-to-date with a Web site by subscribing to its Web feed, which displays the latest site content.

There are many sites — particularly Web logs, or blogs — where the content changes frequently, although not at a regular interval. For these sites, keeping up with new content can be time-consuming, and it is easy to miss new information.

To solve this problem, many sites now maintain Web feeds, which are also called RSS (Real Simple Syndication) feeds. A *Web feed* is a special file that contains the most recent information added to the site. You can use Internet Explorer to subscribe to a site's Web feed. This makes it easy to view the feed any time you want to see the site's new content.

SUBSCRIBE TO A FEED

1. Navigate to the site with which you want to work.

● If the site has at least one Web feed, the Feeds button becomes activated.

2. Click the drop-down arrow to display the Feeds list.

3. Click the feed you want to view.

Internet Explorer displays the feed.

4. Click Subscribe to this feed.

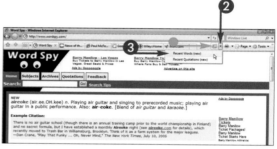

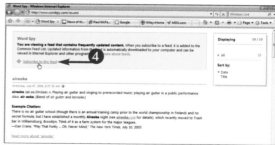

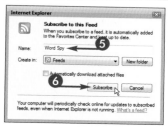

The Subscribe to this Feed dialog box appears.

⑤ Type a new name for the feed (this is optional).

⑥ Click Subscribe.

Internet Explorer subscribes to the feed.

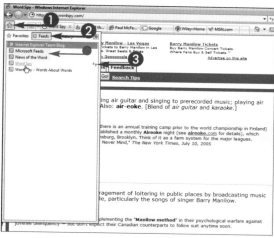

VIEW A FEED

① Click Favorites Center.

② Click Feeds.

● Internet Explorer displays the feeds.

Note: You can also display the Feeds list by pressing Ctrl+J.

③ Click the feed you want to view.

More Options!

Internet Explorer activates the Feeds button when it finds a feed on a site. If you want a stronger indication that a feed is available, click Tools and then click Internet Options to display the Internet Options dialog box. Click the Content tab and then click Settings in the Feeds group. Click the Play a sound when a feed is found for a webpage check box (☐ changes to ☑). Click OK.

You can customize the frequency with which Internet Explorer refreshes a Web feed to suit the way you work or the nature of the feed.

By default, Internet Explorer checks for an updated feed once per day. This is a reasonable schedule for a site that posts new content once or twice a day, or every

couple of days. However, it is not an efficient schedule for feeds that are updated much more or much less frequently. If a feed updates only once a week, checking the feed every day is wasteful for Internet Explorer. You can make a feed more efficient or easier to read by setting up a custom refresh schedule that suits the feed.

① Click Favorites Center.

② Click Feeds.

③ Right-click the feed you want to view.

④ Click Properties.

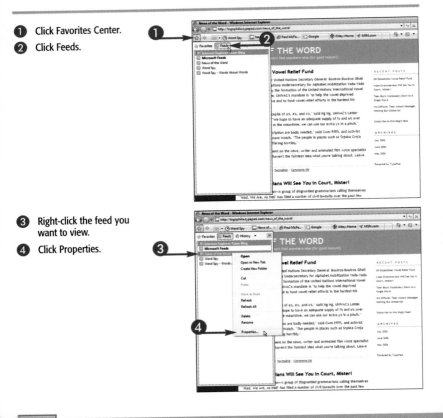

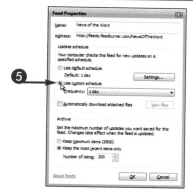

The Feed Properties dialog box appears.

⑤ Click the Use custom schedule option (○ changes to ●).

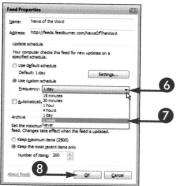

⑥ Click the Frequency list drop-down arrow.

⑦ Click the frequency with which you want to check the feed.

⑧ Click OK.

Internet Explorer updates the feed's refresh frequency.

More Options!

The default interval that Internet Explorer uses to check feeds for new posts is once a day. To change the default schedule, click Tools and then click Internet Options to display the Internet Options dialog box. Click the Content tab and then click Settings in the Feeds group. Use the Default schedule list to click the interval you want to use, and then click OK.

You can make your Web searches more powerful by adding your favorite search engines to the Internet Explorer Search box.

To find the Web site you want, you can take advantage of the various search engines that enable you to find Web pages based on the search text you provide. The Internet Explorer Search box uses the Live Search site to perform its searches.

If you have a search engine other than Live Search that you prefer above all others, you may decide that it is worth the extra effort to navigate to that site rather than using Live Search via the Internet Explorer Search box. However, you can have it both ways. You can configure Internet Explorer to use your favorite search engine via the Search box.

① Click the Search menu.

② Click Find More Providers.

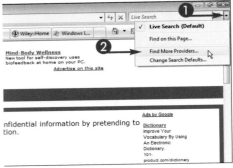

The Add Search Providers to Internet Explorer 7 Web page appears.

③ Click the search engine you want to add to Internet Explorer 7.

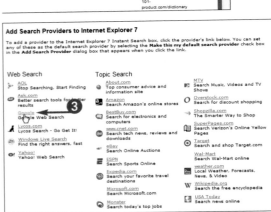

The Add Search Provider dialog box appears.

④ Click Add Provider.

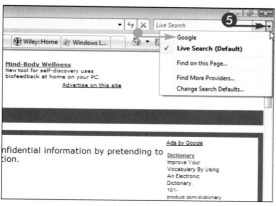

Internet Explorer adds the search engine.

⑤ Click the Search menu.

● The new search engine appears in the Search list. Click the search engine to use it with the Search box.

More Options!

The search engine that Internet Explorer uses in the Search box when you first start the program is called the *default search provider*. The default is Live Search, but you can change it to one of your added search engines. Click the Search menu and then click Change Search Defaults. In the Change Search Defaults dialog box, click the search engine you want to use and then click Set Default. Click OK.

You can customize the Internet Explorer Links bar to provide one-click access to Web sites that you visit most often.

For sites that you visit constantly, the few clicks that it requires to load the sites from the Favorites menu can seem inefficient. For even faster site access, consider the Links bar. This is one of the most useful features of Internet Explorer, but it is also

one of its most hidden. The Links bar, which is turned off by default, is a toolbar designed to hold a collection of buttons, each of which is associated with a Web site. When you click a button, Internet Explorer automatically navigates to the associated site. This gives you one-click access to those sites you visit most often.

DISPLAY THE LINKS BAR

① Right-click an empty section of the Internet Explorer toolbar.

② Click Links.

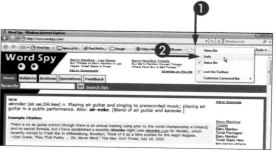

● Internet Explorer displays the Links bar.

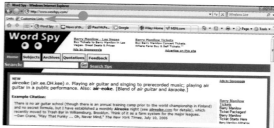

CREATE A BUTTON FOR THE CURRENT WEB PAGE

① Navigate to the page with which you want to work.

② Click and drag the Address bar icon and drop it on the Links bar.

● A new button associated with the page appears on the Links bar. You can click this button to navigate directly to the page.

CREATE A BUTTON FROM A WEB PAGE LINK

① Navigate to the page that contains the link with which you want to work.

② Click and drag the link text and drop it on the Links bar.

● A new button associated with the linked page appears on the Links bar. You can click this button to navigate directly to the linked page.

Customize It!

The positions of the Links bar buttons are not fixed. To move a button to another position, click and drag the button and then drop it in the position you prefer. To rename a button, right-click it, click Rename, type the new name in the Rename dialog box, and then click OK. To delete a button, right-click it, click Delete, and then click Yes when Windows Vista asks you to confirm.

Save Web Sites Longer to Surf More Efficiently

You can improve the efficiency of your Web surfing by increasing the number of days that Internet Explorer maintains a record of the sites you have visited. When you navigate to a Web page, Internet Explorer adds the page's title and address to the History list, which is part of the Favorites Center.

By default, Internet Explorer keeps a page in the History list for 20 days before removing it. However, you may find that you often want to revisit pages after the 20-day period has expired. In that case, you can configure Internet Explorer to save pages in the History list for a longer period. The maximum number of days you can save pages is 999.

---

① Click Tools.

② Click Internet Options.

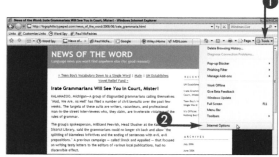

The Internet Options dialog box appears.

③ In the Browsing history group, click Settings.

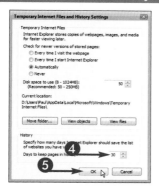

The Temporary Internet Files and History Settings dialog box appears.

④ In the Days to keep pages in history spin box, type or click the number of days for which you want to save Web sites.

⑤ Click OK.

⑥ Click OK.

Internet Explorer puts the new setting into effect.

TIP

Try This!

To work with the History list, click the Favorites Center button and then click History. (You can also press Ctrl+H.) The History list organizes your visited sites into date categories such as Today, Yesterday, Last Week, and Last Month. Click a category, click the site with which you want to work, and then click the specific page you want to visit.

Delete Your Browsing History to Ensure Privacy

To ensure that other people who have access to your computer cannot view information from sites you have visited, you can delete your browsing history. As you visit Web sites, Internet Explorer maintains information about the sites you visit. Internet Explorer also maintains a folder called Temporary Internet Files, which stores copies of page text, images,

cookies, and other content so that sites load faster the next time you view them.

Saving this data can be a problem if you visit financial sites, private corporate sites, or some other page that you would not want another person to visit. You reduce this risk by deleting some or all of your browsing history.

① Click Tools.

② Click Delete Browsing History.

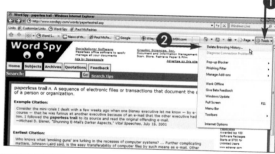

The Delete Browsing History dialog box appears.

③ To delete a specific part of your browsing history, click the appropriate button.

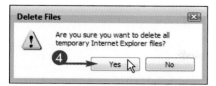

Internet Explorer asks you to confirm.

④ Click Yes.

Internet Explorer deletes the specified browsing history.

⑤ Repeats steps **3** and **4** to delete other parts of your browsing history.

⑥ To delete all of your browsing history, click Delete all.

Internet Explorer asks you to confirm.

⑦ Click Yes.

Internet Explorer deletes all the browsing history and closes the Delete Browsing History dialog box.

● If you did not delete all your browsing history, click Close to exit the Delete Browsing History dialog box.

More Options!

You can control whether Internet Explorer saves your form data as well as your site user names and passwords. Click Tools and then click Internet Options to display the Internet Options dialog box. Click the Content tab and then click Settings in the AutoComplete group. In the AutoComplete Settings dialog box, click to uncheck Forms to stop saving form data. Click to uncheck User names and passwords on forms to stop saving logon data. Click OK.

Chapter 7

Make E-Mail Easier

The World Wide Web may be the most impressive of the Internet services, but it would not be hard to make the case that e-mail is the most indispensable. E-mail, which most of us have been using for only a few years, leaves us wondering how we ever managed without it. E-mail's midway position between conversation and letter writing makes it ideal for certain types of communication, and rarely can a person be found nowadays who does not rely on it.

E-mail is easy to use, but this chapter shows you how to make it even easier. The

tasks you learn here are designed to save precious seconds and minutes of everyday e-mail chores. That may not sound like much, but added up over the course of a busy e-mail day, those seconds can make the difference between leaving work on time and staying late.

Among the timesavers in this chapter, you learn how to leave messages on the server; how to change your message priority; how to create an e-mail distribution list; how to create a backup copy of your address book; and how to spell check your messages.

Quick Tips

You can configure Windows Mail to leave your messages on the server, enabling you to retrieve a message multiple times from different computers.

When you ask Windows Mail to retrieve your messages, it contacts your Internet service provider's e-mail server, downloads the messages, and then deletes them from

the server. However, there may be times when you do not want the messages deleted. For example, if you are working at home or on the road and want to retrieve your work messages, it is better to leave them on the server so that you can also retrieve them when you return to the office.

---

① In Windows Mail, click Tools.

② Click Accounts.

The Internet Accounts dialog box appears.

③ Click the account with which you want to work.

④ Click Properties.

⑤ In the account's Properties dialog box, click the Advanced tab.

⑥ Click the Leave a copy of messages on server check box (☐ changes to ☑).

⑦ Click OK.

⑧ Click Close.

Windows Mail leaves a copy of the messages on the server.

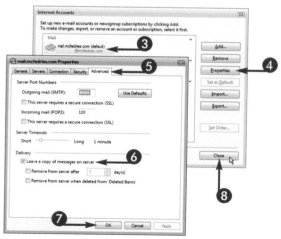

Change Your Message Priority

You can set the priority level of your outgoing message to let the recipient know whether to handle your message with high or low priority.

If you are sending a message that has important information or that requires a fast response, set the message's priority to high. When the recipient receives the message, his or her e-mail program

indicates the high priority. For example, Windows Mail indicates high-priority messages with a red exclamation mark. Alternatively, you can set the priority to low for unimportant messages so that the recipient knows not to handle the message immediately. Windows Mail flags low-priority messages with a blue, downward-pointing arrow.

① In Windows Mail, click File.

② Click New.

③ Click Mail Message.

Note: You can also click Create Mail in the toolbar.

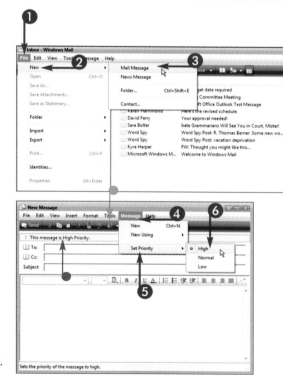

The New Message window appears.

④ Click Message.

⑤ Click Set Priority.

⑥ Click the priority you want to use.

● You can also click Priority in the toolbar.

● When you choose High or Low priority, Windows Mail indicates the current priority level.

E-Mail Multiple People Using a Contact Group

If you regularly send messages to a particular collection of people, you can organize those recipients into a group. This saves time because, when you choose the group as the message recipient, Windows Mail sends the message to every address in the group.

Sending a message to a number of people takes time because you have to either type

many addresses or select many people from your address book. If you find that you are sending some of your messages to the same group repeatedly, you can avoid the drudgery of adding those recipients individually by creating a distribution list or, as Windows Mail calls it, a *contact group*.

---

① In Windows Mail, click Tools.

② Click Windows Contacts.

● You can also click the Contacts toolbar button, or press Ctrl+Shift+C.

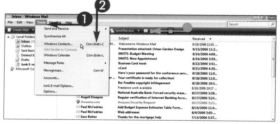

The Contacts window appears.

③ Click New Contact Group.

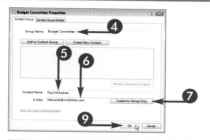

The group's Properties dialog box appears.

④ Type the name of the group in the Group Name text box.

⑤ Type the name of a person you want to add to the group in the Contact Name text box.

⑥ Type the person's e-mail address in the E-mail text box.

⑦ Click Create for Group Only.

⑧ Repeat steps **5** to **7** to add other members of the group.

⑨ Click OK.

● The group name appears in the Contacts window.

Note: If you do not see the group at first, press F5 to refresh the Contacts window.

⑩ Click the Close button to close the Contacts window.

More Options!
If some or all of the people you want to add to the group are already listed in your Contacts list, you can use an easier method to add them to the group. In the group's Properties dialog box, click Add to Contact Group to open the Add Members to Contact Group dialog box. For each person you want to add, press and hold down Ctrl and click the person's name. Click Add when you are done.

Protect Your Contacts by Creating a Backup Copy

You can create a backup copy of your contacts. If you have a problem with the contacts in the future, you can restore your contacts from the backup copy.

The usefulness of the Windows Vista Contacts folder extends far beyond e-mail. For each contact, you can also store data such as his or her home and business addresses, phone and cell numbers, spouse and children's names, birthday, and more.

If you rely on the Contacts folder to store data about the people you know, then you must ensure that the data is safe. Unfortunately, Contacts is just a folder, and if that folder becomes corrupted, you could lose all your contact data. You can protect that data by regularly creating backup copies of your Contacts folder.

---

① In Windows Mail, click File.

② Click Export.

③ Click Contacts.

The Export Windows Contacts dialog box appears.

④ Click CSV (Comma Separated Values).

⑤ Click Export.

The CSV Export dialog box appears.

⑥ Type the location and name of the exported file.

Note: *Be sure to add .csv to the end of the exported filename.*

⑦ Click Next.

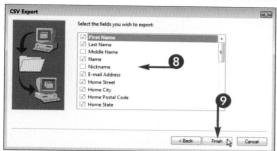

⑧ Click the check boxes for each field you want to include (☑) or exclude (☐).

⑨ Click Finish.

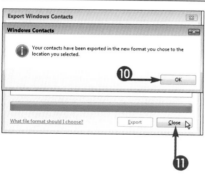

Windows Mail exports the Address Book data to the file.

● The progress of the export is shown here.

⑩ When the export is complete, click OK.

⑪ Click Close.

Important!

If you have a problem with your Contacts folder — for example, if it does not open or does not display your contacts — you can restore it by importing the backed-up copy. In Windows Mail, click File, Import, and then Windows Contacts. Click CSV (Comma Separated Values), and then click Import. Type the location and name of the exported file from step **6** and click Next. Click Finish.

E-Mail an Electronic Business Card

You can create an electronic version of a business card that includes your name, address, and contact information. You can then attach this business card to your messages, enabling other people to add you to their address books more easily.

An electronic business card is called a *vCard* and, just like its paper counterpart,

it includes the person's name, address, phone numbers, and other contact information. If you have an item in the Contacts folder for yourself, you can use it to create a vCard, which you can then attach to your messages. The recipient can then view the attached card and easily add you to his or her address book.

CREATE YOUR BUSINESS CARD

1. In Windows Mail, click File.

2. Click New.

3. Click Contact.

The Properties dialog box appears.

4. In the First text box, type your first name.

5. In the Last text box, type your last name.

6. In the E-mail text box, type your e-mail address.

7. Click Add.

8. Click the Work tab to specify additional information you want in your electronic business card.

9. Click OK.

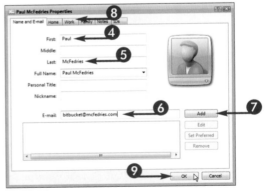

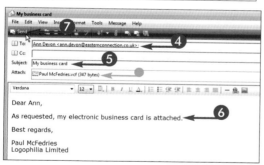

SEND YOUR BUSINESS CARD

1 In Windows Mail, click Contacts.

You can also click Tools and then Contacts or press Ctrl+Shift+C.

The Contacts window appears.

2 Right-click your name.

3 Click Send Contact.

Windows Mail displays a new message window.

● Your electronic business card file is attached to the new message.

4 Type the recipient's address.

5 Type a subject.

6 Type a message.

7 Click Send.

Windows Mail sends the message with your electronic business card attached.

Try This!

If you want to send your electronic business card with every message, click Tools, Options to open the Options dialog box, and then click the Compose tab. In the Business Cards group, click the Mail check box (☐ changes to ☑), click the drop-down arrow in the Mail list, and then click your name. Click OK.

Change the Location of Your Message Store

You can change the hard drive location that Windows Mail uses to store the contents of your message folders. This is useful if you are running out of space on the current hard drive and need to move the messages to a disk with more free space.

Windows Mail stores the contents of your Inbox, Outbox, Sent Items, Deleted Items, Drafts, and Junk E-mail folders, as well as any new folders you create, in a special hard drive location called the *message store*.

The message store often consumes hundreds of megabytes of disk space. If you are running low on disk space and your computer has another drive with more free space, you can give your message store room to grow by moving it to the other drive.

① In Windows Mail, click Tools.

② Click Options.

The Options dialog box appears.

③ Click the Advanced tab.

④ Click Maintenance.

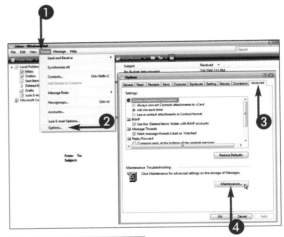

The Maintenance dialog box appears.

⑤ Click Store Folder.

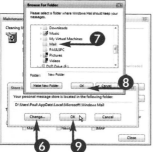

The Store Location dialog box appears.

6 Click Change.

The Browse for Folder dialog box appears.

7 Click the folder you want to use as the new location.

8 Click OK.

9 Click OK.

Windows Mail tells you to restart the program to put the new store location into effect.

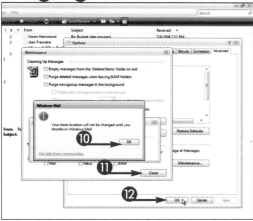

10 Click OK.

11 Click Close.

12 Click OK.

13 Click Close to shut down Windows Mail and then restart the program.

Windows Mail moves the message store.

Important!

To speed up the process of moving the message store, you can compact your folders to remove wasted space caused by message deletions. Follow steps **1** to **4** to display the Maintenance dialog box. Use the Compact the database on shutdown every X runs spin box to specify a relatively small number of runs, such as 10 or 20; the default is 100. Click Close and then click OK.

Activate the Spell Checker to Eliminate Message Errors

You can make your e-mail messages easier to read and more professional in appearance by using the Windows Mail built-in spell checker to catch and fix spelling errors.

Whether you use e-mail for short notes or long essays, you can detract from your message if your text contains more than a few spelling errors. Sending a message riddled with spelling mistakes can also

reflect poorly on you, whether the recipient is your boss, your colleagues, a customer, or a recruiter.

To ensure your message is received in its best light, you should activate the Windows Mail spell checker. This tool then checks your text for errors each time you send a message, and it offers suggested replacements.

ACTIVATE THE SPELL CHECKER

1 Click Tools.

2 Click Options.

The Options dialog box appears.

3 Click the Spelling tab.

4 Click the Always check spelling before sending check box (☐ changes to ☑).

5 Click OK.

Windows Mail activates the spell checker.

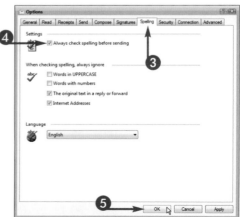

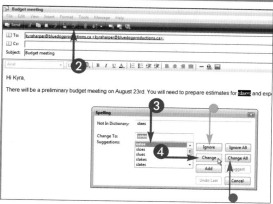

CHECK MESSAGE SPELLING

1. Start a new message and type the body text.

2. Click Spelling.

   If Windows Mail finds a word that it does not recognize, it displays the Spelling dialog box.

3. Click the correction you want to use.

4. Click Change.

● If the word is correct, click Ignore to continue the spell check.

● If the mistake occurs multiple times in the message, click Change All, instead.

5. Repeat steps **3** and **4** for any other words flagged by the spell checker.

   When the spell check is complete, Windows Mail displays a dialog box to let you know.

6. Click OK.

More Options!

The spell checker often flags a word that you know is correct. This can happen with people's names, company names and products, jargon terms, and so on. If Windows Mail flags such a word, you can prevent it from flagging the word in the future by clicking Add in the Spelling dialog box.

You can define a Windows Mail rule by creating the rule from an existing message. In Windows Mail, you use rules to examine incoming messages to set certain conditions. For example, if a message has a particular word or phrase in the Subject line or body, you can move the message to a special folder.

Perhaps the most common rule condition is to use the e-mail address of the sender.

You can redirect the message to a folder for that person's messages, send out an automatic reply, or even automatically delete the message if it comes from someone from whom you do not want to have contact.

With Windows Mail, you can quickly define such rules by creating them from an existing message.

① Click the message from which you want to create the rule.

② Click Message.

③ Click Create Rule From Message.

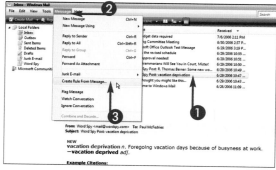

The New Mail Rule dialog box appears.

● Windows Mail automatically activates the Where the From line contains people condition.

● The sender's e-mail address appears in the Rule Description box.

④ Click an action to perform on messages from this address.

⑤ If the action requires more data, click the underlined placeholder.

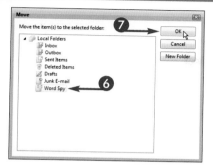

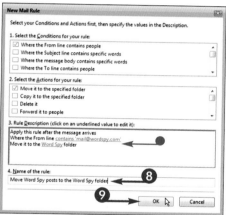

Windows Mail displays a dialog box so you can specify a value for the placeholder. Note that the dialog box you see depends on the action you chose in step **4**.

⑥ Click the data (or, in some cases, type the text) to specify the placeholder value.

⑦ Click OK.

● Windows Mail fills in the placeholder value.

⑧ Type a name for the rule.

⑨ Click OK.

⑩ When Windows Mail tells you the rule was added, click OK.

TIP

Apply It!
After you create the rule from the message, Windows Mail does not apply the rule right away. To apply the rule, click Tools, Message Rules, and then Mail. In the Message Rules dialog box, click Apply Now, click the rule you created, and then click Apply Now.

Synchronize a Newsgroup to Read Posts Offline

You can save connection time by synchronizing a newsgroup so that some or all of its posts are downloaded to your computer. You can then disconnect and read the posts at your leisure.

When you synchronize a newsgroup, you have three choices that govern what you download. The All Messages option means you download every available message, which is useful for newsgroups

that have only a moderate number of messages. The New Messages Only option means you download only those messages posted since the last time you synchronized. Finally, the Headers Only option means you download just the message headers, the sender's address and the Subject line, which is useful for newsgroups with a large number of messages. You can then select individual messages to download.

SYNCHRONIZE A NEWSGROUP

① Click the newsgroup you want to synchronize.

② Click Tools.

③ Click Synchronize Newsgroup.

The Synchronize Newsgroup dialog box appears.

④ Click the Get the following items check box (☐ changes to ☑).

⑤ Click the synchronization option you want to use (◯ changes to ⦿).

⑥ Click OK.

Windows Mail synchronizes the newsgroup.

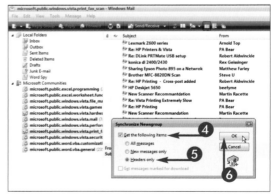

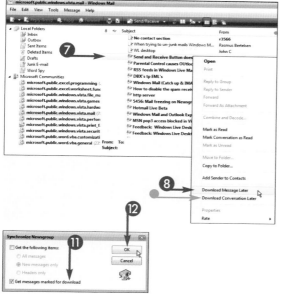

DOWNLOAD MESSAGES

7 If you chose the Headers Only synchronization, right-click a message that you want to download.

8 Click Download Message Later.

● If you want to download the message and all of its responses, click Download Conversation Later, instead.

9 Repeat steps **7** and **8** for other messages you want to download.

10 Follow steps **1** to **3** to display the Synchronize Newsgroup dialog box.

11 Click the Get messages marked for download check box (☐ changes to ☑).

12 Click OK.

Windows Mail downloads the marked messages.

More Options!

If you find that Windows Mail always downloads the messages no matter what synchronization setting you use, click Tools and then Options to display the Options dialog box. Click the Read tab and then click the Automatically download message when viewing in the Preview Pane check box (☑ changes to ☐). Click OK.

Enhance Your Computer's Security and Privacy

These days you may be used to thinking that threats to your computer-related security and privacy come only from the Internet. That is not surprising, because the very real threats of e-mail viruses, system intruders, and identity thieves receive the lion's share of press coverage.

However, many security experts believe that most violations of security and privacy occur not remotely from the Internet, but locally, right at your computer. That is, computer security and privacy are compromised most often by someone simply sitting down at another person's machine while that person is not around.

Windows Vista offers a reassuringly large number of tools and features that you can use to lock up your computer. In this chapter, you learn about most of these tools, many of which are quite simple to implement. Techniques such as adding a password to your account, putting your screen saver in security mode, and clearing your list of recently used documents and media files are all easy to set up, but provide greatly enhanced security and privacy. You also learn more advanced techniques that take security to the next level, including using advanced file permissions and preventing other people from even starting your computer.

Quick Tips

Protect a File or Folder with Permissions

You can use file permissions to specify which users of your computer can access which folders. *Permissions* specify exactly what the groups or users can do with the contents of the protected folder. There are six types of permissions.

With Modify permission, users can view folder contents, open and edit files, create new items, delete files, and run programs. With Read and Execute permission, users can view folder contents, open files, and run programs. With List Folder Contents permission, users can view the folder contents. With Read permission, users can open files, but cannot edit them. With Write permission, users can create new files and subfolders, and open and edit existing files. Finally, with Full Control permission, users can perform any of the above actions and change permissions.

① In a folder window, right-click the folder that you want to protect.

② Click Properties.

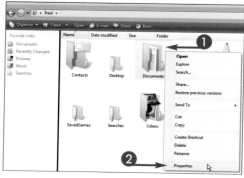

The folder's Properties dialog box appears.

③ Click the Security tab.

● The Group or user names list displays the current groups and users that have permissions for the folder.

Note: *The name in parentheses takes the form COMPUTER\Name, where COMPUTER is the computer's name and Name is the user or group name.*

④ Click Edit.

⑤ Click Add.

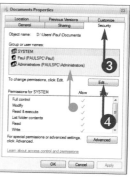

The Select Users or Groups dialog box appears.

6 Type the name of the group or user with whom you want to work.

Note: *If you are not sure about a name, click Advanced and then Find Now. Windows Vista displays a list of all the available users and groups. Click the name you want in the list and then click OK*

7 Click OK.

● The user or group appears in this list.

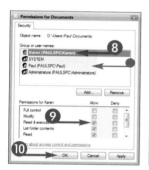 

8 Click the new user or group to select it.

9 In the Allow column, click each permission that you want to allow (☑) or disallow (☐).

10 Click OK.

11 Click OK.

Windows protects the folder with the permissions you selected.

More Options!
You can override a user's group permissions by clicking the corresponding check boxes in the Deny column (☐ changes to ☑). For example, to prevent a member of the Administrators group from viewing the contents of your folder, click the List Folder Contents in the Deny column check box (☐ changes to ☑).

Add a Password to Your User Account

You can configure your Windows Vista user account with a password. Another person cannot log on to your account unless he or she knows the password.

In most cases, when you start your computer, you are taken directly to the Windows Vista desktop. Unfortunately, this enables a system snoop to start your machine while you are not around. With full access to the system, the snoop can

install a virus or a program that monitors your keystrokes to grab your passwords. It is also easy for the intruder to root around in your files looking for sensitive information or even to trash your precious data.

The first and most important step towards preventing all of this is to protect your user account with a password.

---

① Click **Start**.

② Click **Control Panel**.

The Control Panel window appears.

③ Click **Add or remove user accounts**.

Note: If the User Account Control dialog box appears, click Continue or type an administrator password and click Submit.

The Manage Accounts window appears.

④ Click the account to which you want to assign a password.

The Change an Account window appears.

⑤ Click Create a password.

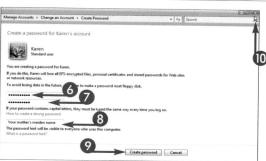

The Create Password window appears.

⑥ Type your password.

⑦ Type your password again.

⑧ Type a word or phrase as a hint.

⑨ Click Create password.

Windows adds the password to the account.

⑩ Click Close to shut down the Change an Account window.

Important!

When you choose a password, select one that is difficult for another user to guess, but one that you can remember. Here are some ideas:

- Do not use obvious passwords such as your name or your birth date.

- Use a password that is at least eight characters long.

- Because Windows Vista passwords are case-sensitive, mix uppercase and lowercase letters.

- Do not write down or tell anyone your password.

Require Ctrl+Alt+Delete Before Logging On

You can configure Windows Vista to require users to press Ctrl+Alt+Delete before they can log on to your computer. This prevents a malicious program activated at startup from capturing your password.

Hackers have figured a way around the user account password system. The trick is that they install a virus or Trojan horse program that loads itself when you start your computer. This program then displays a *fake* version of the Welcome screen. When you type your user name and password into this dialog box, the program records it and your system security is compromised.

To thwart this clever ruse, Windows Vista enables you to configure your system so that you must press Ctrl+Alt+Delete before you can log on. This ensures that the authentic Welcome screen appears.

---

① Click Start.

② Click All Programs.

Note: After you click All Programs, the name changes to Back.

③ Click Accessories.

④ Click Run.

The Run dialog box appears.

⑤ In the Open text box, type control userpasswords2.

⑥ Click OK.

Note: If the User Account Control dialog box appears, click Continue or type an administrator password and click Submit.

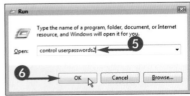

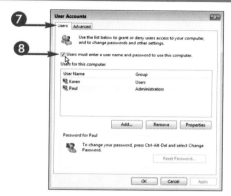

The User Accounts dialog box appears.

7 Click the Users tab.

8 Click the Users must enter a user name and password to use this computer check box (☐ changes to ☑).

9 Click the Advanced tab.

10 Click Require users to press the Ctrl+Alt+Delete check box (☐ changes to ☑).

11 Click OK.

Windows now requires each user to press Ctrl+Alt+Delete to log on.

Did You Know?

When you are logged on to Windows Vista, you can use Ctrl+Alt+Delete to change your user account password. Press Ctrl+Alt+Delete to display the Windows Security window, and then click Change a password. Type your old password, your new password (twice), press Enter, and then click OK.

Lock Your Computer to Prevent Others from Using It

You can lock your computer to prevent another person from working with your computer while you are away from your desk.

Security measures such as advanced file permissions rely on the fact that you have entered the appropriate user name and password to log on to your Windows Vista account. In other words, after you log on, you become a "trusted" user. For more information, see the section "Protect a File or Folder" with Permissions.

However, if you remain logged on to Windows Vista when you leave your desk, another person can take advantage of your trusted-user status to view and work with secure files. You can prevent this by locking your system before leaving your desk. Anyone who tries to use your computer must enter your password to access the Windows Vista desktop.

LOCK YOUR COMPUTER

① Click Start.

② Click Lock.

Note: *You can also press the Windows Logo+L keys. Alternatively, press Ctrl+Alt+Delete and then click Lock Computer.*

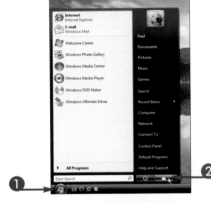

The Windows Vista Welcome screen appears.

● The word Locked appears below your user name.

UNLOCK YOUR COMPUTER

① Click inside the Password box.

② Type your password.

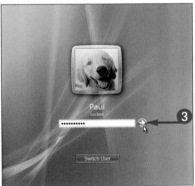

③ Click Go.

The Windows Vista desktop appears.

More Options!

Windows Vista also locks your computer when the screen saver kicks in. If this often happens while you are at your desk, you might want to turn off this feature. Click Start, Control Panel, Appearance and Personalization. Click Screen Saver, and then click the On resume, display logon screen check box (☑ changes to ☐). Click OK.

You can configure Windows Vista to require the insertion of a special floppy disk in your computer before starting up. Without the floppy disk, Windows Vista does not allow anyone to log on to the computer.

Windows Vista stores passwords in encrypted form and uses a system key to decrypt the passwords. This system key is stored on your computer, and if the system key were lost, you would not be able to start your computer.

Therefore, to make sure that no unauthorized user can start your computer, you can move the system key to a floppy disk. If the floppy disk is not inserted into the computer at startup, Windows Vista does not allow anyone to log on to the system.

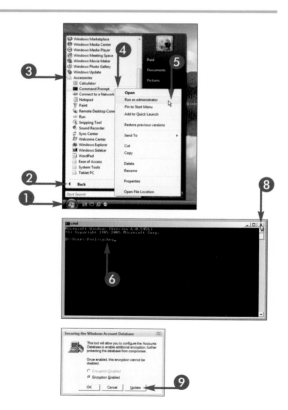

① Click Start.

② Click All Programs.

③ Click Accessories.

④ Right-click Command Prompt.

⑤ Click Run as administrator.

Note: *If the User Account Control dialog box appears, click Continue or type an administrator password and click Submit.*

The Command Prompt window appears.

⑥ Type syskey.

⑦ Press Enter.

⑧ Click Close to shut down the Command Prompt window.

The Securing the Windows Account Database dialog box appears.

⑨ Click Update.

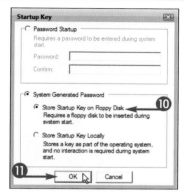

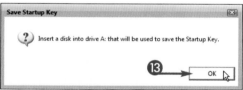

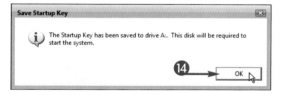

The Startup Key dialog box appears.

⑩ Click the Store Startup Key on Floppy Disk option (◯ changes to ◉).

⑪ Click OK.

The Save Startup Key dialog box appears.

⑫ Insert a floppy disk into your computer's floppy disk drive.

⑬ Click OK.

Windows Vista saves the startup key to the floppy disk and then displays a confirmation dialog box.

⑭ Click OK.

The Success dialog box appears.

⑮ Click OK.

Windows now requires the floppy disk that contains the startup key to log on.

Caution!

After saving the startup key to the floppy disk, Windows Vista looks for the disk when you start your computer. If Vista does not find the key, the Windows Vista Startup Key Disk dialog box appears. You must insert the disk and then click OK. If you lose or damage the disk, you cannot start Windows Vista, so keep the disk in a safe place. Also, be sure to make a backup copy of the disk.

To enhance your privacy, you can clear the Start menu's Recent Items list and Media Player's list of recently played media files.

The Start menu's Recent Items list stores the last 15 documents you have worked on. However, if you know that someone else is going to be using your computer, you may not want the user to see what is on your Recent Items list. To prevent this, you can clear the list.

Windows Media Player maintains a list of files that you have played recently, and it keeps track of the addresses of Internet media you have recently opened. If someone else is going to use Windows Media Player on your computer, you can maintain your media privacy by clearing all this stored information.

CLEAR THE RECENT ITEMS LIST

① Click Start.

② Right-click Recent Items.

③ Click Clear Recent Items List.

● Windows Vista clears the My Recent Items List.

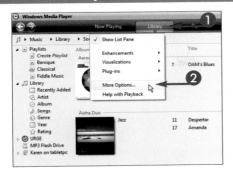

CLEAR RECENT MEDIA

1 In Windows Media Player, click the Library menu.

2 Click More Options.

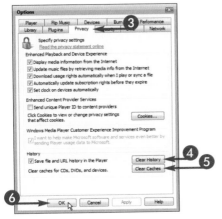

The Options dialog box appears.

3 Click the Privacy tab.

4 Click Clear History to clear the list of recently viewed media files and Internet addresses.

5 Click Clear Caches to clear the downloaded information about audio CDs and DVDs.

6 Click OK.

Windows Media Player no longer lists your recently used media files or Internet addresses.

More Options!
You can configure Windows Vista not to save recently used documents. Right-click Start, click Properties, and then click the Store and display a list of recently opened files check box (☑ changes to ☐). In the Media Player Privacy tab, click the Save file and URL history in the Player check box (☑ changes to ☐).

You can prevent damage from some types of malicious programming by activating a feature that stops those programs from running code in protected portions of your computer's memory.

Windows Vista reserves some of your computer's memory as *system memory*, meant for use by Windows itself. When programmers code software, they usually include fixed-size memory locations called *buffers* that hold data. Unfortunately, a hacker can create a program that deliberately produces a *buffer overrun*: A piece of data larger than the buffer size is loaded into the buffer. The extra data spills over into the system memory, which can then crash or damage the system or even run malicious code.

Windows Vista includes a feature called Data Execution Prevention (DEP) that prevents buffer overruns, and so protects your computer from these attacks.

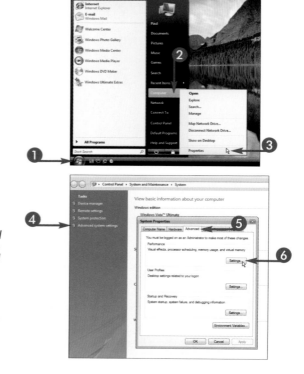

① Click Start.

② Right-click Computer.

③ Click Properties.

The System window appears.

④ Click Advanced System Settings.

Note: *If the User Account Control dialog box appears, click Continue or type an administrator password and click Submit.*

The System Properties dialog box appears.

⑤ Click the Advanced tab.

⑥ In the Performance group, click Settings.

The Performance Options dialog box appears.

⑦ Click the Data Execution Prevention tab.

⑧ Click the Turn on DEP for all programs and services except those I select option (◯ changes to ◉).

⑨ Click OK.

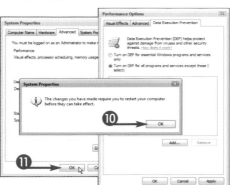

Windows Vista warns you that you must restart your computer to put the change into effect.

⑩ Click OK.

⑪ Click OK.

⑫ Restart your computer.

Windows applies Data Execution Prevention to all your programs.

More Options!
If you have trouble running a program when DEP is on, and your system is virus-free and no program update is available, you can turn off DEP for that program. Follow steps **1** to **8** and then click Add. Use the Open dialog box to display the program's folder, click the executable file that runs the program, and then click Open.

If you share files with other network users, you can configure Windows Vista to control which users can access your files and what actions they can perform on those files.

If your computer is part of a network, it is common to give other users access to some of your files by sharing one or more folders with the network. By default, Windows Vista runs the Sharing Wizard when you opt to share a folder. The Sharing Wizard enables you to set up very simple rules for how users can work with shared folders.

If you want to apply more sophisticated sharing options, such as the folder permissions discussed in "Protect a File or Folder with Permissions," then you need to switch to Windows Vista's advanced sharing features.

---

① Click Start.

② Click Control Panel.

The Control Panel window appears.

③ Click Appearance and Personalization.

The Appearance and Personalization window appears.

④ Click Folder Options.

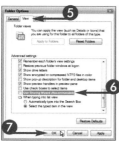

The Folder Options dialog box appears.

⑤ Click the View tab.

⑥ Click the Use Sharing Wizard check box (☑ changes to ☐).

⑦ Click OK.

Windows Vista switches to its advanced sharing options.

Important!

If your computer is part of a workgroup, you can set up an account for each user on every computer in the workgroup. For example, if the user Paul has an account on computer A, you must also set up an account for Paul on computers B, C, and so on. You must assign a password to the account, and you must use the same password for the account on all the computers.

Safeguard Your Computer with a System Image Backup

You can restore your system in the event of a major crash by performing a system image backup using Windows Vista's new Complete PC Backup feature.

PCs can succumb to major calamities, such as a virus or a hard drive failure. In such cases, you often lose access to your entire system.

To make it easier to recover from such a crash, you can create a *system image*

backup, which is a complete backup of your entire system. If you computer crashes, you can restore it to its previous configuration just by restoring the system image backup. Windows Vista enables you to perform such a backup by using its new Complete PC Backup feature, which is only available with Vista Business, Enterprise, and Ultimate.

---

① Click Start.

② Click All Programs.

③ Click Accessories.

④ Click System Tools.

⑤ Click Backup Status and Configuration.

The Backup Status and Configuration window appears.

⑥ Click Complete PC Backup.

⑦ Click Create a backup now.

Note: *If the User Account Control dialog box appears, click Continue or type an administrator password and click Submit.*

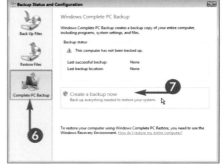

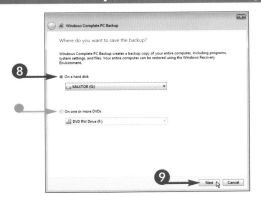

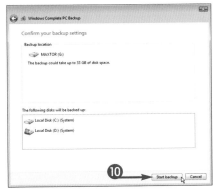

The Where do you want to save the backup? dialog box appears.

⑧ If you want to back up to a hard disk, click the On a hard disk option (○ changes to ◉) and use the list to click the hard disk you want to use.

● To back up to DVD discs, instead, click the On one or more DVDs option (○ changes to ◉) and use the list to click the DVD burner you want to use.

⑨ Click Next.

The Please confirm your backup settings dialog box appears.

⑩ Click Start backup.

Windows Vista backs up your system.

Apply It!

If you need to restore you system, insert your Windows Vista disc, start your computer, wait for the message that prompts you to boot from the disc, and then press any key. When the Install Windows dialog box appears, click Next and then click System recovery options. Click Next, click Next again, and then click Complete PC Restore.

Get More Out of Your Notebook and Tablet PC

Windows Vista comes with many new features for notebook PCs and has support for Tablet PCs built-in to the operating system (except for the Home Basic edition of Windows Vista). If you use a notebook PC regularly, then you will appreciate Windows Vista features such as using an alarm to warn you when your battery power gets low, improving battery life with a custom power plan, and defining what action Windows Vista performs when you press the notebook's power buttons.

Windows Vista also enables you to set up your notebook with a special configuration to use whenever you use your notebook to

give a presentation. For example, you can turn off your screen saver, mute the volume, and pick out a special desktop background.

For Tablet PCs, Windows Vista has many new features, including support for pen flicks, which enable you to navigate your document and perform everyday chores with your digital pen; pen calibration to ensure accurate tapping; a program that lets you capture parts of the screen using your digital pen; the ability to insert handwritten characters automatically; and a system for improving the accuracy of Windows Vista's handwriting recognition.

Quick Tips

You can configure Windows Vista to warn you when your notebook PC battery level is running low so that your computer does not shut down on you unexpectedly. If you are on a plane or in some other location where no AC outlet is available, you have no choice but to run your notebook PC on batteries.

To prevent running out of power, you can configure Windows Vista to display a notification when the battery is low. This warning gives you enough time to save your work and possibly shut down the computer until you can recharge it.

Windows Vista enables you to set the *low battery level*, which is the percentage of remaining battery life that triggers the alarm. The default low battery level is 10 percent.

① Right-click the Power icon in the notification area.

② Click Power Options.

Note: *You can also double-click the Power icon.*

The Power Options window appears.

③ Click Change plan settings.

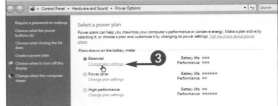

④ Click Change advanced power settings.

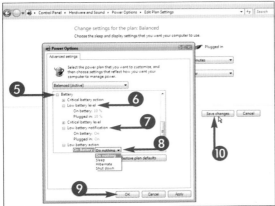

The Power Options dialog box appears.

⑤ Click to expand the Battery branch.

⑥ Click Low battery level, click On battery, and type the percentage at which the low battery alarm triggers.

⑦ Click Low battery notification, click On battery, and click On.

⑧ Click Low battery action, click On battery, and click the action you want Windows Vista to take at the low battery level.

⑨ Click OK.

⑩ Click Save changes.

More Options!

Windows Vista offers three different power plans: Balanced, High performance, and Power saver (see "Create a Custom Power Plan to Improve Battery Life"). You can set a lower power level and low power action for each power plan. Follow steps **1** to **4** to display the Power Options dialog box. Use the power plan list to click the power plan you want to customize, and then follow steps **5** to **9**.

You can improve your notebook PC's battery life or increase your productivity by creating a custom power plan that suits the way you work.

When you use a notebook PC on battery power, you have to choose between increased battery life and computer performance. For example, to increase battery life, Windows Vista shuts down the display and other components after a short time, which reduces performance. Conversely, to increase notebook performance, Windows Vista waits longer to shut down components. These two extremes are controlled by two predefined power plans: Power saver and High performance. The third power plan, Balanced, offers options that strike a balance between battery life and performance.

If none of the predefined power plans is exactly right for you, you can create a custom plan that suits your needs.

① **Double-click the Power icon in the notification area.**

The Power Options window appears.

② **Click Create a power plan.**

The Create a Power Plan window appears.

③ **Click the predefined power plan to use as a starting point option (○ changes to ◉).**

④ **Type a name for your plan in the Plan name text box.**

⑤ **Click Next.**

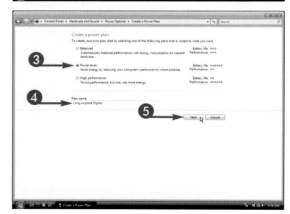

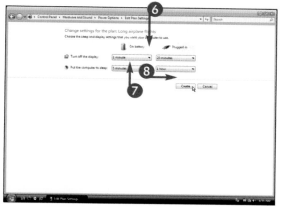

The Edit Plan Settings window appears.

⑥ Under On battery, click the Turn off the display menu arrow to select the idle interval after which Vista turns off the notebook's display.

⑦ Under On battery, click the Put the computer to sleep menu arrow to select the idle interval after which Vista puts the notebook into sleep mode.

⑧ Click Create.

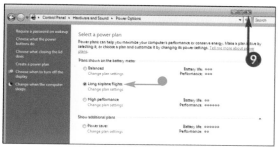

● The Power Options window appears with your custom plan displayed.

⑨ Click Close to shut down the Power Options window.

Delete It!

To remove the custom plan, first change to a different plan by clicking the Power icon and then clicking another plan. Double-click the Power icon to open the Power Options window. Under your custom plan, click Change plan settings, and then click Delete this plan. When Windows Vista asks you to confirm, click OK.

You can activate Windows Vista's notebook power-down modes — shut down, sleep, and hibernate — by configuring your notebook's power buttons.

In shut down mode, Windows Vista closes your open programs and shuts off every computer component. The notebook uses no power while shut down.

In sleep mode, Windows Vista saves all open programs and documents to memory, and turns off everything but the memory chips.

In hibernate mode, Windows Vista saves your open programs and documents to a file, and then shuts down. The notebook uses no power while it is off.

Most notebooks enable you to configure three "power buttons": the on/off button, the sleep button, and closing the lid, and activating these buttons puts your system into shut down, sleep, or hibernate mode.

① Click the Power icon in the notification area.

② Click More power options.

Note: You can also double-click the Power icon.

The Power Options page appears.

③ Click Choose what the power buttons do.

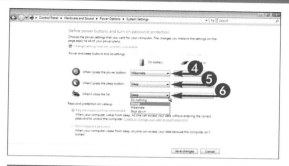

The System Settings window appears.

④ Under On battery, click the When I press the power button menu arrow to select Sleep, Hibernate, or Shut down.

⑤ Under On battery, click the When I press the sleep button menu arrow to select Do nothing, Sleep, or Hibernate.

⑥ Under On battery, click the When I close the lid menu arrow to select Do nothing, Sleep, Hibernate, or Shut down.

⑦ Repeat steps **3** to **5** for the lists in the Plugged in column.

⑧ Click Save changes.

Windows Vista puts the new power button settings into effect.

More Options!

By default, the options in the Password protection on wakeup section are disabled. This security feature forces Windows Vista to display the logon screen when your computer resumes from sleep or hibernate mode. If security is not a concern, you can enable the Don't require a password option by first clicking the Change settings that are currently unavailable link. If you see the User Account Control dialog box, click Continue or type an administrator's password and click Submit. You can now click Don't require a password (○ changes to ◉).

If you use your notebook computer to make presentations, you can configure Windows Vista to use settings that ensure Vista does not interfere with your presentation.

If you use a notebook computer to show a presentation, the computer may get in the way. For example, your computer may display a notification that you have received a new e-mail message.

You can solve such problems by activating an option that tells Windows Vista you are currently giving a presentation. Windows Vista automatically keeps the computer awake and turns off system notifications. You can also configure Windows Vista to disable the screen saver and the desktop background while you are presenting.

① Click Start.

② Click Control Panel.

The Control Panel window appears.

③ Click Mobile PC.

The Mobile PC window appears.

④ Click **Adjust settings before giving a presentation.**

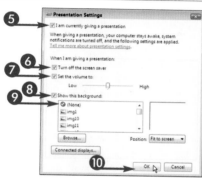

The Presentation Settings dialog box appears.

⑤ Click the I am currently giving a presentation check box (☐ changes to ☑).

⑥ Click the Turn off the screen saver check box (☐ changes to ☑).

⑦ If you want to set the presentation volume, click the Set the volume to check box (☐ changes to ☑) and then click and drag the slider.

⑧ Click the Show this background check box (☐ changes to ☑).

⑨ Click None.

⑩ Click OK.

Important!

Windows Vista remembers your settings, so as long as you do not need to change your setup, in the future you can follow just steps **1** to **5** and then click OK. Note that each time you complete a presentation, you also need to follow just steps **1** to **5** to turn off the I am currently giving a presentation check box (☑ changes to ☐).

If you are using your Tablet PC's digital pen, you can make it easier to navigate and edit documents by activating the Windows Vista new pen flicks option.

Windows Vista enables you to navigate a document using pen flicks. These are gestures that you can use in any application to scroll or navigate. To scroll up, move the pen straight up; to scroll down, move the pen straight down; to navigate

backward in Internet Explorer or Windows Explorer, move the pen straight left; to navigate forward, move the pen straight right.

The pen flicks feature also supports the following editing gestures: Copy (move the pen up and to the left); Paste (up and to the right); Delete (down and to the right); and Undo (down and to the left).

① Click **Start**.

② Click **Control Panel**.

The Control Panel window appears.

③ Click **Mobile PC**.

The Mobile PC window appears.

④ Click Turn pen flicks on and off.

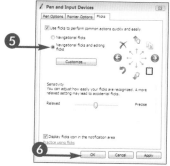

The Pen and Input Devices dialog box appears.

⑤ Click the Navigational flicks and editing flicks option (○ changes to ◉).

⑥ Click OK.

● After you perform your first pen flick, the Pen flicks icon appears in the taskbar's notification area. You can click the icon to see a summary of the pen flicks gestures.

Important!

For a pen flick to work, you need to follow these techniques when performing the gesture: Move the pen across the screen for about half an inch (at least 10mm); move the pen very quickly; move the pen in a straight line; and lift your pen off the screen quickly at the end of the flick.

You can make your Tablet PC digital pen easier to use by calibrating it with your screen.

You can use your Tablet PC's digital pen in the same way that you would use your mouse. That is, you can tap an object to select it, double-tap an object to activate it, tap-and-drag an object to move it, and so on.

However, the usefulness of this feature declines if your digital pen is not calibrated to your Tablet PC screen. This can cause taps and double-taps to occur in places that are slightly off where you intended them to occur. This not only slows you down, but also can cause errors. To prevent this, you need to calibrate your digital pen.

① Click Start.

② Click Control Panel.

The Control Panel window appears.

③ Click Mobile PC.

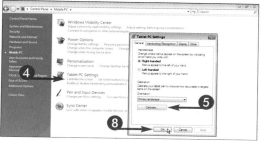

The Mobile PC window appears.

④ Click Calibrate the screen.

The Tablet PC Settings dialog box appears.

⑤ Click Calibrate.

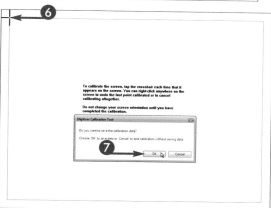

The calibration window appears.

⑥ Tap the middle of the crosshair each time it appears on your screen.

When the calibration is complete, the Digitizer Calibration Tool dialog box appears.

⑦ Click OK.

⑧ In the Tablet PC Settings dialog box, click OK.

More Options!

If you tap the pen, Windows Vista displays an expanding circle at the tap position. If you find this kind of visual feedback distracting, you can turn it off. Follow steps **1** to **3** to open the Mobile PC window, click Pen and Input Devices, click the Pointer Options tab, and then click the check box for each action you no longer want visual feedback for (☑ changes to ☐). Click OK.

You can use the new Snipping Tool to capture part of the screen with your Tablet PC pen and save the result to an image file or Web page.

What do you do if you want to capture part of the screen? For example, you may want to show someone part of a Web site or a dialog box. One solution would be to capture the current screen image by pressing the Print Screen key, opening Paint (or some other graphics program), and then running the Paste command to copy the screen image.

Windows Vista offers an easier method. It is called the Snipping Tool, and it enables you to use your digital pen (or your mouse) to "draw" the area of the screen that you want to capture.

---

① Display the image on screen that you want to capture.

② Click Start.

③ Click All Programs.

④ Click Accessories.

⑤ Click Snipping Tool.

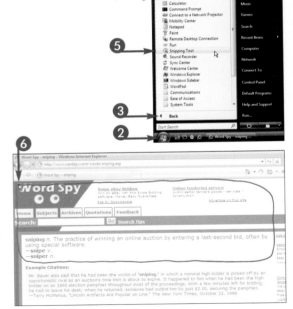

The Snipping Tool window appears.

⑥ Use your digital pen to draw the area of the screen that you want to capture.

A red line shows you the boundaries of the snip.

Note: The Snipping Tool window disappears temporarily from the screen as you draw the clip.

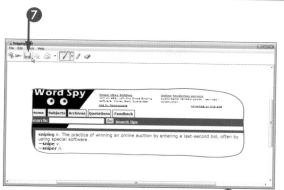

The Snipping Tool window appears and displays the snip.

⑦ Click Save Snip.

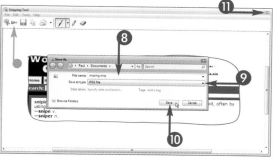

The Save As dialog box appears.

⑧ Type a name for the snip file.

⑨ Click the Save as type menu arrow and select the file type you want to use.

⑩ Click Save.

● To save another snip, display the new object you want to capture, click New, and then follow steps **6** to **10**.

⑪ Click Close.

More Options!

You can annotate the snip before you save it or send it. To write text on the snip, click Tools, click Pen, and then click a pen color. Use your digital pen to write your text on the snip. If you want to highlight snip text, click Tools, click Highlighter, and then drag the digital pen across the text. You can also click Tools and then Eraser to erase any annotations that you added.

You can greatly improve the accuracy of Windows Vista's handwriting recognition by configuring Windows Vista automatically to learn your handwriting style and your vocabulary.

The convenience and usefulness of handwritten text is directly related to how well the Windows Vista recognition feature — called the *handwriting recognizer* — does its job. If it misinterprets too many characters, you will spend too much time either correcting the errors or scratching out sections of text and starting again.

You can greatly improve the accuracy of the handwriting recognizer by configuring Windows Vista to learn how you handwrite text. This Automatic Learning feature does two things: It examines your handwriting style, and it keeps track of words you use in e-mail messages to increase the recognizer's dictionary.

---

① Click Start.

② Click Control Panel.

The Control Panel window appears.

③ Click Mobile PC.

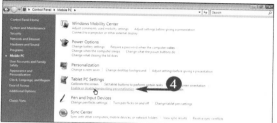

The Mobile PC window appears.

④ Click Enable or disable handwriting personalization.

⑤ Click the Use automatic learning option (○ changes to ⊙).

⑥ Click OK.

Windows Vista enables the Automatic Learning feature.

Try This!

Windows Vista also comes with a personalized handwriting recognition tool that enables you to further improve the accuracy of the handwriting recognizer. Click Start, All Programs, Tablet PC, Personalize handwriting recognition. This displays the Handwriting Personalization window, which takes you through extensive exercises to target specific recognition errors and to teach the recognizer your handwriting style.

Maximize Windows Vista Networking

Most computers today do not operate in isolation. Instead, they are usually connected by one method or another to form a network. If you use your computer in a corporate or small business setting, then your network probably consists of computers wired together through devices such as hubs, switches, and routers. If you use your computer at home, then your network probably consists of computers connected wirelessly through a wireless access point.

Whatever the configuration of your network, it usually takes a bit of extra effort to get the network working smoothly and to ensure that users can access network resources. The tasks in this chapter can help you get the most out of your network. You learn how to view the current network status; how to repair problems; how to customize your network name; how to share folders with other network users and how to protect those folders with advanced permissions; how to create a basic network between two computers with special devices such as hubs or access points; how to connect to a wireless network; and how to change the order of your wireless connections.

Quick Tips

You can make sure your network is operating at its most efficient by checking its current status from time to time.

Networks are generally quite reliable, and you can often go for long periods without any problem. Of course, networks are not perfect, so slowdowns, outages, glitches, and other problems are bound to arise occasionally.

You can anticipate potential problems and gather troubleshooting information by viewing the network status. The status tells you the most basic piece of information you require: whether the computer has a connection to the network. Beyond that, the status also tells you how long the computer has been connected to the network, how fast the network connection is, and for a wireless network, the strength of the wireless signal.

① Click Start.

② Click Control Panel.

The Control Panel window appears.

③ Click View network status and tasks.

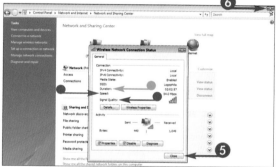

The Network and Sharing Center window appears.

④ Click View Status.

Note: *If you have both a wired and wireless connection, the Network and Sharing Center shows both connections, usually called Local Area Connection and Wireless Network Connection.*

The Wireless Network Connection Status dialog box appears.

● Duration tells you how long this computer has been connected to the network.

● Speed tells you the current network connection speed.

● Signal Quality tells you the strength of the wireless signal (the more green bars you see, the stronger the connection).

⑤ Click Close.

⑥ Click the Close box.

More Options!

On occasion, you may need to know your computer's current IP (Internet Protocol) address, which is a unique value that identifies your computer on the network. To see your computer's current IP address, follow steps **1** to **4** to display the network connection's Status dialog box. Click Details to display the Network Connection Details dialog box, and then read the IPv4 Address value. Click Close.

Run the Network Diagnostics Tool to Repair Problems

If you have trouble with your network, Windows Vista comes with a diagnostics tool that can examine your network and then offer solutions.

Despite the simple networking interface that Windows Vista presents to you, networks are complex structures with many different hardware and software components. If just one of those components becomes unstable, you may encounter network problems. For example, you may no

longer be able to log on to a network or you might not be able to access shared network resources.

When network problems occur, troubleshooting them is often quite difficult. Fortunately, Windows Vista comes with a tool called Windows Network Diagnostics that automates the process. It analyzes many different aspects of your network setup, and then offers solutions you can try.

---

① Click the Network icon.

② Click Network and Sharing Center.

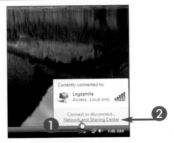

The Network and Sharing Center window appears.

③ Click Manage network connections.

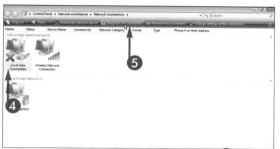

The Network Connections window appears.

Windows Vista indicates the non-working network connection by adding a red X to the connection's icon.

④ Click the network connection that is not working.

⑤ Click Diagnose this connection.

The Windows Network Diagnostics dialog box appears.

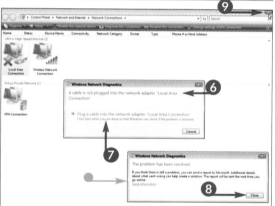

⑥ Implement the solution suggested by Network Diagnostics.

⑦ Click the solution.

Note: *If the solution does not work, Network Diagnostics may suggest other solutions.*

● Windows tells you if the suggested solution works.

⑧ Click Close.

⑨ Click the Close box.

More Options!
If you have multiple network adapters in your computer, Windows Vista sets up in the Network Connections window an icon for each adapter. You may need to test your network connections separately. The easiest way to do that is to disable all but one connection in the Network Connections window, and then run your tests. To disable a connection, follow steps **1** to **3**, click the connection you want to disable, and then click Disable this network device.

Personalize Your Network Name and Icon

You can make the Network Center easier to navigate and you can help to differentiate between multiple networks by personalizing the network names and icons.

When you set up a network, Windows Vista gives the network a default name and icon that appear in the Network Center. The name is either a generic name

such as Network or the default name that the network administrator has set up in a router or gateway device.

If you find yourself working in the Network Center window frequently, you may find the window easier to navigate if you assign names that are more meaningful to each network. This can also help you differentiate between networks.

---

① Click the Network icon.

② Click Network and Sharing Center.

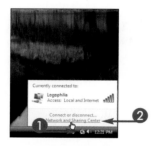

The Network and Sharing Center window appears.

③ Click Customize.

The Set Network Location dialog box appears.

4 In the Network text box, type the new network name.

5 Click Change.

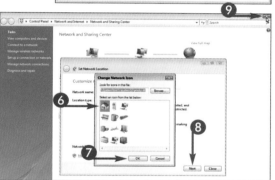

The Change Network Icon dialog box appears.

6 Click the icon you want to use.

Note: To see more icons, type the following addresses into the Look for icons in this file text box:

%SystemRoot%\system32\imageres.dll

%SystemRoot%\system32\shell32.dll

7 Click OK.

8 Click Next.

9 Click Close.

10 Click the Close box.

Important!

The Personalize Settings dialog box also displays the current category of the network. There are three categories: Private (used by home and small business networks), Public (used with networks available in public places such as coffee shops and airports), and Domain (used by corporate networks). Make sure your home or small business network is *not* set as Public. If it is, follow steps **1** to **3**, click Private, click Next, enter your credentials, and then click Close.

You can gain easier access to a shared network folder by displaying the folder as though it were a disk drive on your computer.

You can use the Network window (click Start and then Network) to view the computers that are part of your network workgroup. If you want to work with a shared folder on one of these computers, you must open the computer that

contains the folder, and then open the folder.

Navigating a number of folders every time you want to work with a shared resource is inefficient. To save time, Windows Vista enables you to display any shared network folder as though it were a disk drive on your computer. This is called *mapping* the network folder.

① Click Start.

② Click Computer.

③ Press Alt.

● The Classic menu bar appears.

④ Click Tools.

⑤ Click Map Network Drive.

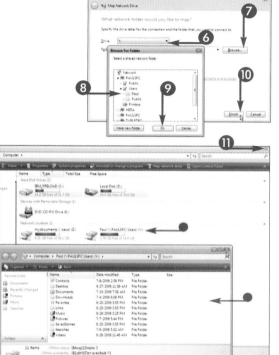

The Map Network Drive dialog box appears.

6 Click the Drive menu arrow and select the drive letter you want to use for the mapped network folder.

7 Click Browse.

The Browse For Folder dialog box appears.

8 Click the network folder you want to use.

9 Click OK.

10 Click Finish.

● Windows Vista opens a new window to display the contents of the mapped folder.

● An icon for the mapped folder appears in the Network Location section of the Computer window.

11 Click the Close box.

Note: To avoid conflicts with the drive assignments that Windows Vista supplies for removable memory cards, use higher drive letters (such as X, Y, and Z) for your mapped network folders.

Remove It!

To speed up the Windows Vista startup and reduce clutter in the Computer window, you can disconnect mapped network folders that you no longer use. To disconnect a mapped folder, click Start and then Computer. In the Network Location section, right-click the network drive you want to disconnect and then click Disconnect. If Windows Vista asks you to confirm, click Yes.

You can allow users to work with some of your documents by sharing a folder with the network.

The purpose of most networks is to share resources between the computers connected to the network. For example, the users on a network can share a single printer or an Internet connection. This resource sharing also applies to documents, for example, a presentation that you want other people to comment on or a

worksheet that you want people to modify. In all these cases, the easiest way to give other people access to your documents is to share the document folder with the network.

To follow the steps in this task, you need to deactivate the Windows Vista Sharing Wizard, as described in "Switch to Advanced Sharing to Improve Security" in Chapter 8.

---

① Open the folder that contains the folder you want to share.

② Right-click the folder you want to share.

③ Click Share.

You can also click the Share button in the taskbar.

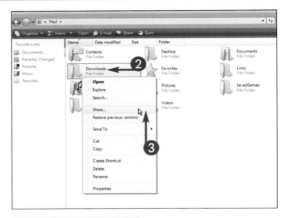

The folder's Downloads Properties dialog box appears.

④ Click Advanced Sharing.

Note: *If the User Account Control dialog box appears, click Continue or type an administrator password and click Submit.*

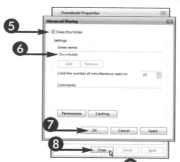

The Advanced Sharing dialog box appears.

5 Click the Share this folder check box (☐ changes to ☑).

6 Edit the Share name, if desired.

7 Click OK.

8 Click Close.

● Windows Vista adds the sharing icon to the shared folder's existing icon.

Note: *If you do not see the sharing icon right away, press F5 to refresh the window.*

9 Click the Close box.

Note: *This task shows you how to set up basic folder sharing. To learn how to protect your shared folders with permissions see "Protect Your Files with Advanced File Permissions."*

More Options!
If you want to change the share name of your folder, first follow steps **1** to **4** to display the Advanced Sharing dialog box. Click Add to display the New Share dialog box, type the new share name you want to use, and click OK. Use the Share name list to click the old share name and then click Remove. Click OK and then click OK again.

Protect Your Shared Files with Advanced File Permissions

You can use file permissions to specify which network users can access which folders, and what exactly those users can do with the files in those folders.

Windows Vista enables you to set permissions for folders that you have shared with the network. Permissions specify exactly what specified users or groups can do with the contents of the protected network folder. In this case, there are three types of permissions.

With Full Control permission, network users can perform any of the actions listed. Network users can also change permissions. With Change permission, network users can view the folder contents, open files, edit files, create new files and subfolders, delete files, and run programs. With Read permission, network users can open files but cannot edit them.

① Follow steps **1** to **4** in the preceding task to open the Sharing dialog box.

② Click Permissions.

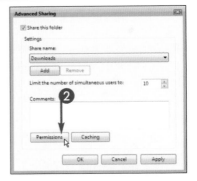

The folder's Permissions for Downloads dialog box appears.

③ Click Add.

Note: For extra security, make sure you do not give the Everyone group Full Control or Change permission.

The Select Users or Groups dialog box appears.

④ Type the name of the group or user with which you want to work.

⑤ Click OK.

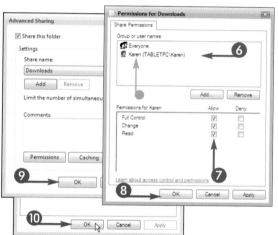

● The user or group appears in this list.

⑥ Click the new user or group to select it.

⑦ In the Allow column, click each permission that you want to allow (☑) or disallow (☐).

⑧ Click OK.

⑨ Click OK.

⑩ Click OK.

Windows protects the folder with the permissions you selected.

More Options!
By default, Windows Vista allows only people who have a user account on your computer — or people who know a user name and password on your computer — to access your shared folders. To change that, click the Network icon in the taskbar's notification area, and then click Network and Sharing Center. In the Sharing and Discovery section, click On beside the Password protected sharing item. Click Turn off password protected sharing (○ changes to ◉), click Apply, and then enter your credentials.

Work with Network Files Offline

You can work with network files and folders even when you are not connected to the network.

You can still get network access of a sort when you are disconnected from the network, or *offline*. Windows Vista has an Offline Files feature that enables you to preserve copies of network files on your computer. You can then view and work with these files as though you were connected to the network.

When you reconnect to the network, Windows Vista automatically *synchronizes* the files. This means that Windows Vista does two things: First, it updates your offline files by creating copies of any new or changed files in the shared network folder. Second, it updates the shared network folder with the files you changed while you were offline.

① Click Start.

② Click Network.

The Network window appears.

③ Double-click the network computer with which you want to work.

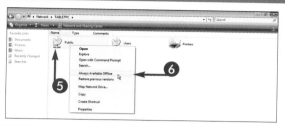

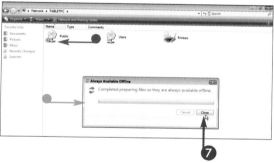

The network computer's shared resources appear.

④ If the files you want to use offline are in a subfolder, click the folders until you see the subfolder you want.

⑤ Right-click the folder you want to use offline.

⑥ Click Always Available Offline.

Windows Vista makes local copies of the folder's files.

● The Always Available Offline dialog box appears.

⑦ Click Close.

Note: The Always Available Offline dialog box closes itself automatically after a few seconds.

● Windows Vista adds the Sync icon to the folder's regular icon.

You can now use the folder's files even when you are disconnected from the network.

Important!
When Windows Vista synchronizes your offline files, it may find that a file has been changed both on the network share and on your offline computer. In that case, the Sync Center reports that the "Sync failed" and displays a "conflict" link. Click that link, click the conflict, and then click Resolve. The Resolve Conflict dialog box gives you three options: keep the offline version of the file (you lose the network changes); keep the network version of the file (you lose your offline changes); or keep both versions (the offline version is saved under a modified filename).

Manually Connect to a Hidden Wireless Network

If a nearby wireless network is not broadcasting its identity, you can still connect to that network by entering the connection settings manually.

Each wireless network has a network name — often called the Service Set Identifier, or SSID — that identifies the network to wireless devices and computers with wireless network cards. By default, most wireless networks broadcast the network name so that you can see the network and connect to it. However, some wireless networks disable network name broadcasting as a security precaution.

You can still connect to a hidden wireless network by entering the connection settings by hand. You need to know the network name, the network's security type and encryption type, and the network's security key or passphrase.

① Click Start.

② Click Connect To.

The Connect to a network window appears.

③ Click Set up a connection or network.

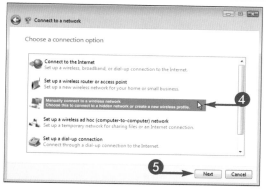

The Choose a connection option window appears.

④ Click Manually connect to a wireless network.

⑤ Click Next.

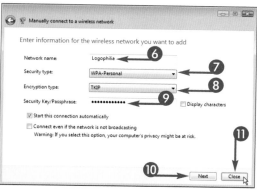

⑥ Type the Network name.

⑦ Click the Security type menu arrow to select the network's security type.

⑧ Click the Encryption type menu arrow to select the network's encryption type (if any).

⑨ Type the network's Security Key/Passphrase.

⑩ Click Next.

Windows Vista connects you to the network.

⑪ Click Close.

Caution!

Activating the Connect even if the network is not broadcasting check box could create a security problem for your network. The problem is that your computer will send out probe messages looking for the network if it is not broadcasting. These messages include the name of the network. This is a security risk, because a person with the right equipment can intercept those messages and learn the name of the hidden wireless network.

Index

Index